TO

FROM

DATE

100 DAYS OF strength IN ANY STRUGGLE

A DEVOTIONAL JOURNAL

(in)courage

A DaySpring COMMUNITY

100 Days of Strength in Any Struggle: A Devotional Journal

First Edition, January 2024

Published by:

DaySpring

21154 Highway 16 East
Siloam Springs, AR 72761
dayspring.com

Written by: (in)courage
Cover Design by: Hannah Brinson

Printed in China
Prime: U1605
ISBN: 979-8-88602-519-4

Introduction

You can't do this life on your own . . . and you're tired of trying. You need evidence that God is still present and good when everything around you tries to convince you otherwise. You need help and encouragement to keep going when the one next step is simply too much. We get it.

What if you could actually see God clearer and know Him deeper in the middle of your struggles? What if you don't have to muster up more grit, determination, and wisdom on your own but could tap into the source of true, unfailing strength? Here's the good news: You can.

You are stronger than you think because God is closer than you know.

100 Days of Strength in Any Struggle will take you on a journey of learning to see God clearer and to know Him deeper in the middle of your struggles. As you experience pain, move through daily challenges, or get bogged down by anxieties big or small, you'll learn to find Him right in the middle of it, ready to strengthen you and give you rest.

These 100 devotions from the writers of (in)courage provide life-line Scriptures and real-life stories to help you grow stronger with Jesus one step at a time. Every day you'll be prompted to write down where you are finding God's strength. No answer is too small. You might find God's strength in a song, a sunset, or a timely text message from a friend. By intentionally looking for God's strength every day, at the end of your journey you'll be able to look back and see 100 ways God's strength met you and sustained you even if your circumstances didn't change.

You'll be reminded that you were never alone and that God is stronger than you imagined—and so are you.

REMEMBERING GOD

Strong Enough to Lean In

BY ANNA E. RENDELL

In the last few months, I've had a fractured elbow, a gum tissue graft, and a massive, infected cyst removed from my neck. I've been miserable, in pain, and rendered helpless at some points along the way.

I'm not used to asking for help, accepting care, and taking a break, and these past few months, I've had to do all of the above. My husband faithfully bandaged, unpacked, cleaned, and rebandaged the surgical site on my neck. My daughter brushed my hair while my arm was wrapped in a sling. My friend sent coffee money when the baby stopped sleeping and my mouth—swollen and stitched—could only handle icy liquids.

While I am not great at accepting it all, I'm learning that in a way, being dependent is a good thing. My friend calls it being "strong enough to lean." And so, lean I will, right into the arms that hold the strongest. I'm learning to lean in, depend on, and accept the care God offers me all the time. And that care reminds me of a mom.

God wants to care for us like the best mother there ever was—ready to help put our minds at ease, invite us to practices that help our whole selves, and/or give us a kick in the pants to shake it off and get moving. Maybe a combination of it all because that might be what we really need.

Just as the best mother ever constantly thinks about and cares for her children, God does the same for us. He cares for us, and He'd like us to care for ourselves too. That care might look like a doctor's appointment to check on that weird thing, or like drinking that glass of water, or going to bed early, or praying when you're worried. It might also look like accepting help from a friend, admitting when things are a big deal and when we need to be taken care of.

Let's be strong enough to lean in—to God and others—and let's do what we need to do to take care of ourselves well.

Day 1

"AS A MOTHER COMFORTS HER CHILD,
SO WILL I COMFORT YOU."

Isaiah 66:13 NIV

TODAY, I AM FINDING GOD'S STRENGTH IN

REMEMBERING GOD

When You Feel Unseen

BY ANJULI PASCHALL

I noticed my soul was feeling unseen. I can always tell when I'm weary by how I respond to simple requests. Today, I was annoyed. Too little time. Too many needs. Too few "thank-yous." I just felt like a means to an end. I was at everyone else's disposal. *Mom, get me that! Mom, where is my homework? Mom, why are we having that for dinner again?* I'm tired of running on everyone else's timeline and to-do list. I'm pouring out constantly with little input coming back.

Then this text came in: "I forgot my sports stuff. Bring it."

Not even a "please," I thought to myself. I huffed as I grabbed his bag, angrily throwing it into the car and driving across town during school traffic. My son met me at the front office with a half-smile. With staff and students surrounding us, I handed him his bag, and we made quick small talk. He's almost a head taller than me now. He turned away. I turned away. Seven steps later I heard him shout, "I love you, Mom."

Tears brimmed my eyes. I didn't dare turn around and embarrass him by weeping in front of all his people. But as soon as I got into the car, I bawled. I've become so bitter. I've become someone I don't want to be—always agitated and on edge. Someone who rushes and dismisses and rolls my eyes, forgetting why I do any of this at all—it's for love.

But even as I forget, the love of God reaches into my weariness . . . my resistance . . . my tiredness. In the most unexpected moments and surprising places, God reminds me that I'm seen and the people in my life really do care.

God sees me, and He sees you too. In a crowd of busy high school kids, God did an intervention through my son's three words. It wasn't magical; it was unmerited favor. That's the grace of God—ready to reach into your ordinary life too.

Day 2

SHE GAVE THIS NAME TO THE LORD WHO SPOKE TO HER: "YOU ARE THE GOD WHO SEES ME," FOR SHE SAID, "I HAVE NOW SEEN THE ONE WHO SEES ME."

Genesis 16:13 NIV

TODAY, I AM FINDING GOD'S STRENGTH IN

REMEMBERING GOD

God Is with You in the Storm

BY BARB ROOSE

One afternoon, I left home for a brief walk. The gusting winds should have prompted me to turn around, but I pressed on. The sun was out, and the weather was uncharacteristically warm, so I was surprised when big, springtime raindrops began dotting the ground around me.

Getting out of the rain wasn't an option. As the clouds rolled across the sky into a charcoal gray, I hustled back toward home. My hoodie and pants collected heaven's water, making each step a little heavier and more uncomfortable to take. The rain had only begun minutes before, but I wanted out. Storms are uncomfortable. They make us think scary thoughts. Every few steps, I'd glance up at the sky, entertaining catastrophic thoughts like what would happen if lightning struck while my keys were in my pocket.

As the fear of the storm nipped at my heart and fast-falling raindrops puddled around my feet, I was reminded of the promise that no matter what I face, God is always with me.

The storms of life often catch us unaware. The rains of life fall on us all. It's not a punishment from God, rather a reality of living in our fallen world. As much as we want out of the storm, God knows that we get stronger when we endure through it with Him by our side.

When the storm feels unbearable, remembering these truths will help you get through it:

You are not alone. *Take a next step.*

God is with you and for you. *Take one more step.*

Your storm won't last forever. *You can do this.*

Don't let fear make you forget God's promises. *Keep going until you get through it.*

Day 3

"WHEN YOU GO THROUGH DEEP WATERS,
I WILL BE WITH YOU."

Isaiah 43:2 NLT

TODAY, I AM FINDING GOD'S STRENGTH IN

Sitting in the Tension of Gratitude and Grief

BY JEN SCHMIDT

With her father by her side, my niece floated down the stairs and then stepped toward her future groom. Long before my brother knew the name of his daughter's future spouse, he had been praying about the possibility of this day. From start to finish, it was the glorious affirmation of all they'd prayed for.

But my weekend also included one of life's greatest sorrows—the tragic loss of my dear friend's child. I was at my niece's rehearsal dinner when I received the text. On the other end of the phone, my friend's heart was splayed open from the devastation of her loss. Her daughter was gone too soon, never to have a rehearsal dinner or first dance.

As I texted my grieving friend on the morning of the wedding, I shared that while I'd have to compartmentalize my feelings to celebrate, my heart wouldn't be far from hers. She texted back, "Jen, go rejoice with those who are rejoicing. We will have plenty of time for mourning later."

My memories of that wedding week are so complex, but they've taken me to a deeper level with the Lord than I've experienced in a long time. Though our Lord does graciously give good gifts to His children, we are not guaranteed a life without grief and loss.

I'm choosing to not allow worry to be used as a weapon to harm me. The enemy mentioned in I Peter 5:8 is trying his best, but I'm taking every single worry for myself, for my dear friend and her family, and for our future, and wielding it as worship with my eyes fixed on the only Waymaker.

God is here amidst our laughter and lament, amidst our worry and our worship. I know this to be true, and I will choose to continue to anchor my heart in His Word.

Whatever season you're walking through right now, one thing is certain: God is intricately involved in both our suffering and celebrating—our gratitude and grief. In His goodness, I find grace for myself, and there is grace for you too.

Day 4

REJOICE WITH THOSE WHO REJOICE;
MOURN WITH THOSE WHO MOURN.

Romans 12:15 NIV

TODAY, I AM FINDING GOD'S STRENGTH IN

God's Comfort When Troubles Don't Stop

BY KATHI LIPP

I was behind on everything.

I'd tell myself to just do the next thing or to stop being so lazy.

I finally began seeing a therapist because I had such a hard time functioning. I couldn't be creative or concentrate, and I didn't want to hang out with anyone else besides my husband and my dog.

My therapist asked some initial questions, and I responded with, "Yeah, this thing happened, but it's not a big deal." Or "Yeah, it was hard for me, but other people have had it so much worse . . . "

She finally stopped me and asked, "Have you heard of compound trauma?"

I hadn't. She went on to explain. "Yes, any one of those things on their own may not have sunk you. But what it sounds like is that life has been unrelenting, and each of these traumas—and that's what they are, traumas—has left you without the ability to recover."

And as soon as I heard this, I, a dedicated non-crier, broke down in a flood of tears.

Yes, horrible things have happened to others, and I will mourn with them. But the magnitude of someone else's suffering does not lessen my suffering. And until I allow myself to grieve, I cannot recover.

So many of us have been through surprisingly hard things. It doesn't matter if other people are tougher than you. It doesn't matter if your friend or your neighbor could handle circumstances better than you could. God has made it clear that to be there for others, we must allow God to comfort us. God comforts us through others who are going through similar circumstances—through other people's creative acts of kindness. Through the Word, prayers, and the love of the people God has surrounded us with, we feel His comfort.

He calls Himself the God of all comfort, and He proves that over and over again.

Day 5

BLESSED BE THE GOD AND FATHER OF OUR LORD JESUS CHRIST, THE FATHER OF MERCIES AND GOD OF ALL COMFORT, WHO COMFORTS US IN ALL OUR AFFLICTION, SO THAT WE MAY BE ABLE TO COMFORT THOSE WHO ARE IN ANY AFFLICTION, WITH THE COMFORT WITH WHICH WE OURSELVES ARE COMFORTED BY GOD.

II Corinthians 1:3–4 ESV

TODAY, I AM FINDING GOD'S STRENGTH IN

Struggle in the Ordinary

BY ANNA E. RENDELL

I work my full-time job from a desk in the corner of my bedroom. Just to the right of my chair is the only full-length mirror in the house. It hangs on my scratched-up, builder-grade closet door and reflects me sitting at my desk. And usually, a kid who comes visiting.

There's laundry piled high on one side of the chair. I don't know if it's dirty or clean—probably both. Until April, there was a Christmas tree peeking out in the corner. I've had the desk chair since college, and my chipped-paint desk was a garage sale find. Packages opened but not dealt with lie just out of my mirror view. Jeans wait in a bag to be returned. Summer activity brochures splay open on the carpet, my desk tasks spilling over onto the floor.

Outside the bedroom/office door, my kids bicker and protest bedtime, and more laundry waits. House projects compel, dishes fill the sink, and the empty fridge reminds me I need to get groceries, stat.

I only must turn around to see the ways I'm behind on life.

My to-do list always overruns the lines on a page, reminding me that it will never end.

It's not hard to get overwhelmed by it all. So many tasks. Some nonnegotiable, others that can (and will) wait. Yet amidst the to-do's engulfing me, there's a tiny nugget of peace when I remember the hands that are truly holding all things together.

When I'm overcome by the tasks and ordinary stuff of my life, even then God is with me. It doesn't require a crisis to be exhausted and in need of God's peace. When we remember to lean into Him instead of fretting over what remains undone, it can seriously strengthen our hearts.

On the overwhelming and ordinary days, He knows our steps, and He walks them with us. The tasks may pile up, but they'll never overtake the love, peace, and strength God has for us.

Day 6

WHEN MY SPIRIT WAS OVERWHELMED WITHIN ME,
THEN YOU KNEW MY PATH.

Psalm 142:3 NKJV

TODAY, I AM FINDING GOD'S STRENGTH IN

It's Okay to Not Be Okay Today

BY KAITLYN BOUCHILLON

I planted my heels firmly into the ground and, with both my hands and my voice shaking, read a prayer to close my grandfather's funeral service. With the wind blowing and tears falling and God watching, I held the prayer written weeks in advance in my hands, printed on a folded piece of paper, and gave the words back to the One who always knew the timeline.

By and large, we are a culture that is uncomfortable with grief—our own as well as the grief of others. I get it; grief is messy. But grief and hope are not mutually exclusive. One does not cancel out the other.

In fact, when I think of those who have walked through difficult times with hope instead of pretending all was okay, it bolsters my faith. Because how else can we say that, but Jesus? There's something strikingly beautiful and outrageously compelling in someone who says, "I'm not okay right now, but I will be, and God is nothing less than faithful."

Hurt is not something to hurry through, and grief is not something you need to get over. You don't need to sweep sorrow under the rug or rush to find beauty in the broken places. You can be sad without shame or a timetable. It's okay to acknowledge what was or wasn't or will never be; to say that, yes, seasons come and seasons go and this will not last forever . . . but for now, the storm's still raging.

One day, there'll be no need for a black dress. One day, every grave will be a garden. One day, we'll build altars in the ruins as we sing songs of praise to the God who redeems and restores all, to the One who even now is making all things new. But for now, let's just pass the tissues. Let's learn to say, "I'm not okay right now, but I will be, and God is nothing less than faithful."

You don't have to hold it together because there is One who is holding you.

Day 7

HE WILL WIPE EVERY TEAR FROM THEIR EYES,
AND THERE WILL BE NO MORE DEATH
OR SORROW OR CRYING OR PAIN.

Revelation 21:4 NLT

TODAY, I AM FINDING GOD'S STRENGTH IN

The Fruit of the Struggle

BY LUCRETIA BERRY

After playing the last note to their duet, my daughter shoved the music sheet back toward her big sister and forced herself to take a bow before stomping off the recital stage. As her sister proceeded to play her solo piece, our little girl cried in my arms, defeated and disappointed. Though both girls performed their solos flawlessly, their duet didn't go as well as they had hoped.

When my girls were deflated by their less-than-perfect performance, I realized I had taught them to celebrate success and had failed to teach them to appreciate struggle. Acknowledging struggle is common. Less common is noting and appreciating all the gifts that challenges provide along the way.

I wish I'd thrown a parade for my girls after each practice to mark the accomplishment of a struggle. I wish I'd helped them understand that though the process is ugly, it's the perfect way to help them cultivate all kinds of beauty—beauty like persistence, surrender, patience, grace, teamwork, and sisterhood—regardless of their talent.

Sometimes, during struggle, we lose sight of God's presence, of what God is showing us about ourselves, of the divine purpose in the process. We don't have to be afraid of struggle, nor do we have to struggle in fear. God has auspiciously entwined struggle, reward, and fruit. They are inseparable. I have learned to express gratitude for each. In so many of life's circumstances, struggle can be the more significant, enduring reward.

I'm getting better at celebrating during struggle, and I'm teaching my children to do the same. Fortunately, I'm sure life will give us many more opportunities to practice.

We all know struggle and the disappointment of failed expectations. We've all felt discouraged, defeated, and deflated when an outcome isn't what we had hoped. But we can know that because God is with us in the midst of our struggle, we don't have to be afraid, and our labor is not in vain. We can face the struggle expecting to learn, grow, and gain immeasurably.

Day 8

"HAVE I NOT COMMANDED YOU?
BE STRONG AND COURAGEOUS. DO NOT BE AFRAID;
DO NOT BE DISCOURAGED, FOR THE LORD YOUR GOD
WILL BE WITH YOU WHEREVER YOU GO."

Joshua 1:9 NIV

TODAY, I AM FINDING GOD'S STRENGTH IN

Seeing the Full Picture When We Look Back

BY MARY CARVER

This was the year I dreaded buying Christmas cards. Because you can search every shelf, but you won't find one that reads, "Joy to the Lord! This year I doubted God!"

For the first time in my life, I had questioned God's goodness. I questioned His sovereignty. I questioned my own adherence to beliefs that weren't doing a thing in the face of a particular grief. I also published two books, took a spontaneous road trip with my husband and kids, and survived working from home while also helping my daughters do school at home.

How could all of that be true at the same time? In the same year? How could a big, wonderful, beautiful year also contain some serious anguish and doubt that shook me to my core? How could one small season hold the weight of enormous blessings and crushing burdens?

I'm not sure how it's possible, but I know it's true. All the amazing things that happened aren't less real or less valuable because of my struggle. And the fact that I wrestled with my faith in a new and painful way wasn't reduced by the fact that I experienced a lot of joy. Our lives are full of both joy and pain—often at the very same time. And that's okay. We can acknowledge both. We can hold both.

And we can worship God through both.

The good parts of the year are actually richer because of the thread of pain and doubt and struggle that winds through the weeks and months. Only by seeing the good and the hard intertwined and overlapping do I see how faithful God has been to me.

He's not just here when you're happy. He's not just here when you're grateful. He's not just here when you're rock solid, believing with all your heart. He's here, always, no matter what. He's here no matter how much your circumstances, your life, or your heart change. He's here, and He never changes.

Day 9

JESUS CHRIST IS THE SAME YESTERDAY, TODAY, AND FOREVER.

Hebrews 13:8 NLT

TODAY, I AM FINDING GOD'S STRENGTH IN

What to Do When You Get Wound Up

BY MELISSA ZALDIVAR

I meet with a spiritual director every month. She's a Jesus-loving woman who sits down with me and helps me sort through things. As we dug in one day, I felt in my gut a whole lot of things rising to the surface. There was anxiety and insecurity and anger and sadness and confusion that had been bubbling for a long while without me even knowing, and I found myself getting, well, wound up. *What do I do next? What am I supposed to be doing now? Am I in the right place? Is my calling something else?*

The questions kept winding me up tighter and tighter until she gently asked me to take some deep breaths and pray.

Ten minutes later, I let out a sigh and said, "What I need is a getting ready for God's best for me; instead, I was rushing ahead without intentionally turning my attention to Jesus and tuning into His voice."

I recalled how a baseball pitcher moves his body intentionally to create forward motion and pitch the ball where it needs to go. We call it "the windup." Similarly, I found myself desiring to be intentional in my efforts with Jesus and leaning into whatever He had for me. But I almost missed it because I wasn't getting ready for God's best for me; instead, I was rushing ahead without intentionally turning my attention to Jesus and tuning into His voice.

I wasn't giving myself space to unwind either—to sit down and rest with God, allowing His voice to fill the quiet places. I longed to just sit with Him and let the fears and concerns go for a moment.

So often, we live in the place of getting wound up instead of listening to the call to unwind or wind up. We think we're doing what's good for our hearts, but maybe we're asking the wrong questions or going into a quiet time with a list of things to rant about. Certainly, Jesus can handle our rants. But perhaps when we pause to pray, we can hear God better than when we wind ourselves up.

Jesus can carry us, friend. Go find Him, wind up and unwind.

Day 10

"COME TO ME, ALL YOU WHO ARE WEARY AND BURDENED, AND I WILL GIVE YOU REST."

Matthew 11:28–29 NIV

TODAY, I AM FINDING GOD'S STRENGTH IN

Nothing Is Bigger Than God

BY SIMI JOHN

Last fall, I started having some breast pain that took me to my family doctor who then ordered a mammogram and an ultrasound to rule out "anything serious." I had no family history of breast cancer, but I had a few friends whose lives had been wrecked by a completely unexpected diagnosis. Proactively, I decided to undergo testing.

While I was at work, I got the call from the cancer center to make the appointment. My heart beating faster, I quickly wrote down the date and time on a sticky note and hung up the phone. I felt the warmth of my tears fall down my cheek. It just became real—the possibility that my life could soon change. I only told a few close friends about it, asking them for prayer.

The week of my appointment I was actually preparing a sermon on joy (my husband and I copastor a church). In fact, we were scheduled to prerecord this message on joy two hours after my appointment. On my way to the cancer center that morning, anxiety overwhelmed me, and I got lost driving to the hospital. I was overwhelmed by the thought that this could be the day that changed my plans, my future, and literally my whole life. As my mind played out all the worst-case scenarios, I sat there trying so hard to cling to the God I know instead of the voice of doubt and fear.

I called my husband and told him that I couldn't speak on joy when I was overcome with so much fear. And he calmly responded, "Simi, this diagnosis may change your life, but it doesn't change your God."

His words shifted something deep within me. I began to remember past circumstances where I faced opposition, rejection, and confusion and how God's goodness and faithfulness saw me through.

He hasn't changed.

I walked into the hospital scared but hopeful, because I knew I wasn't walking in alone. The same God who had always been there for me was with me, even now. Cancer is not bigger than Christ. Indeed, nothing is bigger than God.

Day 11

BUT I HAVE TRUSTED IN YOUR FAITHFUL LOVE;
MY HEART WILL REJOICE IN YOUR DELIVERANCE.

Psalm 13:5 CSB

TODAY, I AM FINDING GOD'S STRENGTH IN

Using God's Presence in the Past to Strengthen Your Faith in the Future

BY MICHELE CUSHATT

I never expected to be mom to six children. I always wanted to be a mom and to have a house full of family members. But SIX? Seems a bit excessive. And yet, here I am, mom to six children between the ages of thirty-one and sixteen. *Lord, have mercy.* I hardly know how I keep track of birthdays let alone all the other details.

Although a full house comes with many benefits, I'm convinced it's to blame for every gray hair. A small fortune covers them up with a nice dark brown, but underneath is an ocean of grey and white, and I've earned every one.

For us, parenting came in two phases: the first three, and then the second three. That means, I currently have three teenagers still at home. This is round two through adolescence, and although I love the teen years for many reasons, it isn't easy. The mood swings. The constant activity. The attitudes and demands. The boyfriends and girlfriends and breakups. Did I mention the mood swings? Then, once they get their driver's license, there is the constant clock-watching and worry until they walk back in the door safely.

Parenting isn't for the faint of heart. And it definitely pushes my aging self to the brink of outright panic at times. However, one truth holds me firm when the weight of the unknown threatens to take me under: the same God who has carried me will also carry them.

His love is unshakeable, His presence inescapable, His grace unstoppable. The same God who has picked me up and put me back together time and time again is able to do the same in my children, whether teenagers or adults. So, although I can't be with them each moment of each day, they are not alone. God is with them. He is with you too.

I may still experience sleepless nights or shed a few tears, but God's presence is my peace in the struggle.

Day 12

"EVEN TO YOUR OLD AGE AND GRAY HAIRS I AM HE, I AM HE WHO WILL SUSTAIN YOU. I HAVE MADE YOU AND I WILL CARRY YOU; I WILL SUSTAIN YOU AND I WILL RESCUE YOU."

Isaiah 46:4 NIV

TODAY, I AM FINDING GOD'S STRENGTH IN

Believing Against Hope That the Harvest Is Coming

BY JEN SCHMIDT

When our son and daughter-in-love found out they had a minute chance of having biological children, we were all devastated. Infertility isn't often addressed from a future grandmother's point of view, but watching your child be filled with such heartbreak and face closed doors is a pain for which I wasn't prepared. Yet amidst such disappointment, the Lord has drawn me closer.

For years I've held our son and daughter-in-love's sorrow near to my heart. I've wrestled hard with the Lord over this diagnosis, and He's okay with that. I'll admit that I've even gotten a little judgy, pointing fingers at others wondering, *Why them and not us?* Yes, these thoughts have bubbled up, yet God welcomes my questions, my cries, and even my dashed dreams.

As the months turned to years, we were invited to claim Galatians 6:9 as our pillar of hope: "Let us not become weary in doing good, for at the proper time we will reap a harvest if we do not give up."

With that goal, I've decided to guide my heart of sadness toward declarations of praise for the Lord's faithfulness and to walk with those journeying through silent suffering. Does this change our kids' prognosis? No. Are there still questions and uncertainty? Absolutely. But I persevere and trust in His goodness. I choose to believe His promise and hope in a plentiful harvest because it will come at the Lord's "proper time." I have no idea what that will look like, but I wait as God continues to write the story for my children.

While He delights in showing His power through miracles, my expectant prayers have shifted: *Lord, please expand their family in any way that brings You the most glory. This is hard, but it's all for You.*

And shouldn't that be our cry every day? With work or neighbors, family or friends? *Show me how to bring You the most glory, Lord. Every single choice is all for You.*

Let's not become weary in our wait. His harvest is coming.

Day 13

LET US NOT BECOME WEARY IN DOING GOOD,
FOR AT THE PROPER TIME WE WILL REAP A HARVEST
IF WE DO NOT GIVE UP.

Galatians 6:9 NIV

TODAY, I AM FINDING GOD'S STRENGTH IN

For Anyone Who Thinks She's Failing

BY JENNIFER DUKES LEE

Many summers ago, according to my to-do list, I was failing.

I had blown so many self-imposed deadlines. Major goals on my list remained unmet. Even small projects around the house were back-burnered. With the kids home, my day was a symphony of constant interruptions, sounding like the clatter of breakfast, the rushing toward music lessons, the whirring of the washing machine.

In an effort to stay sane, I prayed the same prayer every single morning: "God, help me to make choices today that honor Your plans for my life."

I determined to follow God's agenda rather than trying to convince Him to help me carry out mine. This is no small task for a woman with a rather robust inner control freak. There are times when I secretly hope God will empower me to plow through *my* to-do list rather than equip me for *His*.

But God is totally on to me. The old saying, "If you want to make God laugh, tell Him your plans," summed up my summer. Sure, there were moments of terrific productivity. But often, my daily prayer led me miles away from the office.

As it turns out, that summer was exactly what my agenda-driven heart needed. Which is to say, my soul needed a place to breathe. My soul needed days of cute kittens, impromptu picnics with the girls, kayak rides, and petunias—alongside satisfying days of productivity.

I can't simply walk away from my work, of course. But I have surrendered my agenda to the God of The Calendar. I choose to be sustained by the belief that God will help me complete the work He has called me to do . . . *in His time.*

Maybe you've been like me—caught between your grand plans and your actual life. Maybe you've been feeling a little panicky that what you *intended* to do, simply hasn't gotten done. Maybe what we all really need right now is to remember that God has this all under control. We get to simply pray, "God, help me to make choices today that honor Your plans for my life." Amen!

Day 14

YOU CAN MAKE MANY PLANS,
BUT THE LORD'S PURPOSE WILL PREVAIL.

Proverbs 19:21 NLT

TODAY, I AM FINDING GOD'S STRENGTH IN

When It's Been a Lot for What Feels Like a Long Time

BY KAITLYN BOUCHILLON

On an ordinary Tuesday afternoon, I opened my inbox and gasped. Inside, an email invited me to congratulate my grandma on a milestone number of years in her listed profession: pastor's wife. Just past the hilarity of "How in the world is she on LinkedIn and who signed her up?" is the gut punch, the sting of tears, the unexpected wave of sadness rolling in.

What LinkedIn didn't know is that my grandma passed away.

Within my small circle of close friends over the last two years we've walked through death, cancer, car wrecks, job loss, difficulty finding a new job, break-ups, abuse, starting over in a new city, a heartbreaking diagnosis, medical unknowns from the lack of a diagnosis, and unexpected surgeries. It's a lot of loss. It's a lot of grief. It's a lot of change.

It's been a lot for what feels like a long time.

I'm convinced one of the most beautiful verses in all of Scripture is found in John 11:35: "Jesus wept." Despite knowing resurrection was written onto the next page of the story, the Man of Sorrows chose to grieve what was broken. Hope Himself let His heart break, and somehow, it's this that gives me hope during my heartbreak.

Jesus isn't scared of our grief or disappointed that we're still sad; He just comes closer to weep with us. He isn't surprised by our despair or our anger; He gets angry with death, too, lamenting what has broken even though the Word knows the final word belongs to restoration, to the joy that awaits us in heaven.

It's okay if you aren't okay today. It's okay to not be okay tomorrow either. Waves will come—some stronger than others, some seen from a distance—and others will take you completely by surprise. Storms will come, but God's promise to save and redeem those who trust in Him is guaranteed, and His presence is with us always.

Our friend Jesus is acquainted with grief and familiar with waves. We have a God who cries. We have a reason to hope.

Day 15

JESUS WEPT.

John 11:35 NIV

TODAY, I AM FINDING GOD'S STRENGTH IN

Peace in the Middle of the Storm

BY MICHELE CUSHATT

I was fine, totally fine. Or so I thought.

And then after a long day of work and another hour making a home-cooked dinner, one unnamed thirteen-year-old made one too many critical comments, and I went from okay to out-of-control.

Rest and recovery have eluded me recently. There's lots of tension and anxiety and chaos—in my home and in the world. We're like too many passengers, crammed into a too-small dingy, thrust into the wide-open sea and then caught in a furious, terrifying storm. It reminds me of one stormy day when Jesus's friends woke Him up in the boat crying, *"Master, Master, we're going to drown!"* (Luke 8:24 NIV).

I understand the disciples' panic—their ability to go from fine to undone in the span of seconds. My squall may not come in the form of rain and wind, but it's just as terrifying and damaging. And I'm usually the source of its sting—in my impatient responses and curt replies, my critical remarks and unforgiveness. When the tension and anxiety and chaos rise, my peace and self-control go down.

The funny thing about tension, anxiety, and chaos is that the first things we often let go of are what we need the most: quiet, prayer, meditation, Bible reading, solitude. It seems there isn't time or energy for it.

A few days ago, I realized once again how insecure, irritable, and overwhelmed I felt. I was so caught up in the turmoil of the storm I forgot that Jesus was in my boat. To stay afloat, I needed to remember the only One who could offer me true peace.

"Where is your faith?" Jesus asked the disciples (Luke 8:25 NIV). He asks the same of you and me. And for today, I remember that although my world rocks and the wind roars, my faith is with Jesus. He sits in my boat, even while the storm grows. That means my Peace is with me, right here, right now, no matter what comes.

Day 16

"PEACE I LEAVE WITH YOU; MY PEACE I GIVE YOU.
I DO NOT GIVE TO YOU AS THE WORLD GIVES.
DO NOT LET YOUR HEARTS BE TROUBLED
AND DO NOT BE AFRAID."

John 14:27 NIV

TODAY, I AM FINDING GOD'S STRENGTH IN

Wishing for "Normal" and Seeing God's Character

BY JAMI NATO

I knew early on our daughter was different. She wasn't walking. She skipped crawling. I ached when I heard other toddlers forming beautiful little words, like *mama* or *dada*, while she remained silent. It turned out she couldn't hear for the first several years of her life. Fixing her hearing was just the beginning of the long journey of advocating for our daughter.

There are many faith songs about surrendering to God and trusting His plan, but if I'm honest, I'd rather sing those songs than live them. However that's not the call of the faith we profess. We often can't understand what God is doing, but we are called to trust that He knows better and will work it for our good.

There was a time (or seven) in our journey with Lila where I thought I could fix her with the newest therapy, the greatest miracle supplement, or praying hard enough. I have since stopped believing that if she were more "normal," she would have a better life. God didn't make a mistake when He weaved her genes together and made her just so. This leads me to believe He is showing a part of Himself through her.

She watches others open a gift and cries with joy, jumps up and down, and hugs them, as if she were the one receiving it. Give me boundless joy like that! She walks down to the neighbor's house and asks them, with intensity, "And how was your day?" Give me others-centered awareness like that! I almost missed out on God in her by wishing my circumstances were more "normal."

We can have faith that our lives and their interruptions will accomplish God's good purpose. And perhaps, once we start believing this to be true, we can open our white-knuckled grip and receive a better gift than we could imagine: Jesus. It was never about our circumstances. It was always about Him.

Day 17

"FOR AS THE HEAVENS ARE HIGHER THAN THE EARTH,
SO ARE MY WAYS HIGHER THAN YOUR WAYS
AND MY THOUGHTS THAN YOUR THOUGHTS."

Isaiah 55:9 ESV

TODAY, I AM FINDING GOD'S STRENGTH IN

Hope Will Not Put You to Shame

BY ALIZA LATTA

My head had pulsed for thirteen days straight. Nothing seemed to help this migraine. I thought my brain would explode. I cried out to God. "I remember how You've healed people," I prayed, tears coursing down my cheeks. "You can heal my migraine. Nothing is too hard for You."

I fell asleep, expecting my migraine to be gone when I awoke. But it wasn't. When my eyes opened the next day, I waited for a few moments to see if the pain was gone. The migraine gripped me even harder.

I blinked back tears, deeply discouraged. I softly uttered, "Why didn't You heal me, God? I believed You could—I truly believed! Why haven't I been healed?"

I was riddled with anxiety: *What if I have migraines forever? What if I'm never healed?*

I took a deep breath and felt a few words softly make their way across my heart. In my discouragement, I almost didn't notice them. *Have hope.*

Even though my circumstances had not changed, I could still hope . . . even if the hope scared me.

Though I did not understand why He didn't heal me in the timing I wanted, I could hold firm to the promise that my hope was in Jesus and my hope would not put me to shame. So, I started hoping. As I chose hope over discouragement—even though the pain was still there—my mindset changed.

And then, three days later, on day sixteen, after a couple of chiropractic appointments, a lot of prayer, some ice packs, and essential oils, the migraine finally left me.

But I was still left with one thing: hope.

Maybe you, too, need to hope for something. Sometimes it feels scary to hope—because what if God doesn't come through for us? What if this time He forgets? You can rest in the assurance that God never has and never will forget you. You can hope in Him, and He will never put you to shame.

Day 18

AND HOPE DOES NOT PUT US TO SHAME,
BECAUSE GOD'S LOVE HAS BEEN POURED OUT
INTO OUR HEARTS THROUGH THE HOLY SPIRIT,
WHO HAS BEEN GIVEN TO US.

Romans 5:5 NIV

TODAY, I AM FINDING GOD'S STRENGTH IN

When You Face a Terrible Tuesday

BY JEN SCHMIDT

We've all had days when everything goes wrong. Not tragedies, but regular problems strung together to really mess with our attitudes. Welcome to my Terrible Tuesday. Nothing about this day made me want to sing, "This is the day the Lord has made, let us rejoice and be glad in it."

It began at 1:30 a.m. when our college son's shell-shocked voice woke me out of a deep slumber: "I'm okay, but my car is totaled." Hours later, our oven short-circuited while I baked fifty homemade scones for a local coffee shop delivery. Lastly, as I was frantically preparing for my first "Moms Night Out at Jen's" since the COVID quarantine lifted, our well water pump broke. Fifteen young moms were coming in a few hours, and with no running water, that meant no flushing toilets either.

I admit to raising my fist for a brief moment and saying, "Seriously, Lord? In twelve hours, we've had a totaled car, an oven fiasco, and now a broken pump? Can You give me a break?"

I knew how much all the moms had been looking forward to gathering. Friends assured me that everyone would understand if I canceled. Even though I felt defeated, I knew that if this much opposition swirled against our evening, there was no way I could cancel. God was up to something special, so I begged Him to take my terrible Tuesday and transform it into changed lives.

Almost double the moms expected showed up. All evening I took mental snapshots of women laughing, crying, connecting, and even sharing with absolute strangers. Chaos came in, but grace flowed out. Throughout the evening, women hugged my neck, thanked me for not canceling, and told me how it was exactly what their hearts needed.

Kingdom adventure awaits as we shift our focus from "not on this terrible day" to "Yes, Lord, I'm here for it." If I had canceled that evening, I would've missed out on the chance to end the day declaring, "This is the day the Lord has made, let us rejoice and be glad in it!"

Day 19

THIS IS THE DAY THAT THE LORD HAS MADE;
LET US REJOICE AND BE GLAD IN IT.

Psalm 118:24 ESV

TODAY, I AM FINDING GOD'S STRENGTH IN

A Precious Gift in the Middle of Tough Times

BY BARB ROOSE

Everything seemed so bright. We had a wonderful life, complete with happy kids, good salaries, and a hopeful future. But with one crisis after another, that life faded away, leaving behind a pile of debt, unemployment, arguments, and so much anxiety.

What happened to my life, God? Did we do something wrong? Tell me what kind of magic-button prayer will get us out of this mess!

I cried every day. I begged God to rescue us from the land of uncertainty and give us back our old life. I coped with the only strategy I knew: worrying. I thought I could protect myself from more pain if I imagined all the worst-case scenarios in advance: *What if we can't pay this month's bills or the medical test? What if we need a new transmission? What if our life never gets better?* However, obsessing over my "what if" worries didn't make me feel better. Instead, I felt worse!

Maybe you're like me, faced with an uncertain season of life and stuck in the middle of hardship or heartache. Jesus understands. Jesus knew one day His closest friends would be fearful of the future and worries would overwhelm their hearts and minds. So, before His death, He made this promise: *I am leaving you with a gift—peace of mind and heart. And the peace I give is a gift the world cannot give. So don't be troubled or afraid* (John 14:27 NLT)

The peace Jesus gives provides supernatural calm in the midst of chaos and hardship. It's the kind of peace we absolutely need when we're not sure what will happen next.

It took a few years of stressed-out days and sleepless nights for me to learn to surrender my worrying ways in favor of Jesus's peace. Though our difficult season continued, God was faithful to remind me of His promised peace.

We can rest assured that God's promise doesn't have an expiration date. It never runs empty. And when our "what if" worries try to steal our calm, we are only a prayer away from unshakable faith and receiving shalom from the Prince of Peace.

Day 20

"CAN ALL YOUR WORRIES ADD
A SINGLE MOMENT TO YOUR LIFE?"

Matthew 6:27 NLT

TODAY, I AM FINDING GOD'S STRENGTH IN

Am I Making a Huge Mistake?

BY ALIZA LATTA

I sat outside on my apartment balcony, a light breeze wisping strands of hair against my shoulders. My fingers sat atop my laptop keyboard, my heart pounding with every press of the keys. I googled, "How to write a resignation letter" and slowly began crafting my own. Was I making a massive mistake?

I had a clear path in front of me, each rung of the corporate ladder shiny and sparkling above me. I knew I could keep climbing. I could stay comfortable. But the still, small voice inside me was inviting me to leave my job and enter a new season. Truth was, I had no inkling of what that new season might contain. The idea of leaving my job felt akin to jumping off a cliff, and I hadn't a clue what was waiting for me below.

I was an associate producer for the largest news corporation in Canada. Everyone disagreed with my decision to leave. My family. The news corp. Normally when everyone disagrees with me it's a sure sign I ought to listen to their wisdom and not my inner rebel. But it wasn't my inner rebel I was listening to this time . . . it was my Good Shepherd.

I'd fasted and prayed for months. I'd asked a spiritual director to talk me through the decision. And over and over, I kept getting a word from the Holy Spirit: *He was my Rock*. I didn't know what was ahead, but I knew I had a Rock to land on. I was still afraid, but I wanted to trust that God would lead me. He did.

I left the world of news producing and weeks later found myself accepting a job to plant and pastor a small church. I had planned to be a journalist, telling the truth to hundreds of thousands. Now I was a pastor, telling a far greater Truth to a congregation of eighty.

I never thought I'd find myself here. But my Rock did. And in Him, I will always take refuge.

Day 21

THE LORD IS MY ROCK, MY FORTRESS AND MY DELIVERER;
MY GOD IS MY ROCK, IN WHOM I TAKE REFUGE.

Psalm 18:2 NIV

TODAY, I AM FINDING GOD'S STRENGTH IN

Sometimes You Just Need to Trust the Process

BY DORINA LAZO GILMORE-YOUNG

A few months ago, I invited my friend to join me for a pottery class. Our teacher encouraged us to gently nudge the pedal to get the wheel spinning. With wet hands, we learned to center and cone the clay. The process of forming clay on the wheel was longer and harder than it looks. The trick was to keep adding water to keep the clay supple. We pressed, pulled, and pinched until that ball of clay eventually became a bowl or vase.

A few times, the teacher came over, stuck her hands in front of me, and started to work with my clay. At first, I wanted to take control of the clay myself. I wanted to learn by doing it myself. But soon I realized the value in surrendering to her expertise. In fact, I learned a lot from watching my teacher and her techniques.

In the pottery studio, I also learned that pushing on the pedal to speed up the wheel does not actually make the work go faster. I had to be slow, deliberate, and intentional if I wanted to make a beautiful bowl.

It turns out in pottery-making, as in life, you have to trust the process. It's rare that someone would sit down at a pottery wheel and make something perfect on the first try. Oftentimes the clay needs to be reworked, reshaped, and reimagined.

Our lives are like that too. God the Potter can do whatever He wants with us, the clay. He can push out our inconsistencies, transform our too-jagged edges, and smooth us to symmetry. It might feel uncomfortable or too long in the waiting, but we are not to resist His design work. We are to submit to His molding and making, and behold His creative process embodied in us.

After the class, our teacher fired our creations in the kiln. The bowl I made sits on my bathroom counter now, holding some of my favorite jewelry pieces. It's a sweet reminder that God is the Potter, and we are but dust mixed with water in His heart-shaped hands.

Day 22

WE ARE THE CLAY, AND YOU ARE THE POTTER.
WE ALL ARE FORMED BY YOUR HAND.

Isaiah 64:8 NLT

TODAY, I AM FINDING GOD'S STRENGTH IN

A God Who Holds Us

BY HOLLEY GERTH

The sun has long since slipped beneath the horizon, but I'm still at my computer. I'm exhausted, but I push myself to click a few more keys. There was a season in my life when work was like an addiction. It's been years ago now, but I still remember how it wreaked havoc on my life.

No one confronted me about my work habits. I didn't get arrested. I never attended rehab. Instead, I got told, "Good job!" and "Keep at it!" Productivity and busyness gave me a sense of worth; they made me feel needed and valued. I've come to believe anything we consistently do to excess can become a trap.

It doesn't matter if our behavior is labeled "good" or "bad." It's the effect on our lives and relationships that matters. I've seen people become dependent on "good" things like helping, legalism, meeting needs, and religious activities. We all have something we're consistently tempted to numb out to.

We all know what this is like—to live fighting off the urge to have another drink, eat another cookie, say "yes" to one more request, or put in another hour at the office long after we know we should have gone home. The good news is we don't have to win the battle on our own.

This doesn't mean we simply say a prayer and have automatic victory. Getting free may involve counseling, accountability, a support group, many times of trying and failing, as well as practical and spiritual resources. Jesus will empower us to overcome what we're struggling with and help us regain our peace.

When Jesus began to free me from finding my identity in my work, I felt terrified. If I didn't keep up the pace, then surely everything would fall apart. This is what addictive behavior tries to tell us—that if we stop, we will never be okay.

But I discovered when we stop trying to hold it all together, we can finally rest in what we need most—a God who holds us.

Day 23

WHO WILL RESCUE ME FROM THIS BODY THAT IS SUBJECT TO DEATH? THANKS BE TO GOD, WHO DELIVERS ME THROUGH JESUS CHRIST OUR LORD!

Romans 7:24–25 NIV

TODAY, I AM FINDING GOD'S STRENGTH IN

Trust in God Who Holds All Things

BY RACHEL MARIE KANG

"I feel so stupid," I said. Tears gathered in my eyes.

"No," she reassured me. "You're not stupid. You've worked really hard."

"But I've been doing it wrong. I've wasted all this time," I insisted. Then, I sat there, crying in the chiropractor's office.

I have pain that's anchored in the lower left side of my back—a few car accidents, inflammation in the hips, and leg braces as a kid will do that to you. And so, I do everything I can think of to stop this pain and address the root strain from which it all stems. I stretch, I rub peppermint oil, I research, I drink water, I pray, I supplement, and I shell out money I do not have for the relentless rounds of chiropractic appointments, week after week after week after week. I do everything in my power to not only heal the pain, but to also prevent and alleviate the strain it will put on my body in years to come.

Only now, I am beginning to see a trend in this train of thought: I want to fix broken things and, deeper still, I want to prevent things from breaking. And I crumble, altogether fall apart, anytime I realize I cannot fix everything . . . nor can I, in fact, prevent things (like my body) from breaking or failing or persisting with pain.

This is when I need the reminder to relinquish my control, to put my trust in God who holds all things in His hands—all hurt, healing, hardship, and hope. This is when I want to fall deeper into trust with God as I make peace with His power and the reality of His all-knowing and all-powerful nature.

At one point or another, there comes the time to release our limited capacity and reorient to the truth of God's limitless strength and power. It comes time to catch sight of His supreme authority, the fact that He is capable, is in control, and cares for and about us more than we ever could.

Day 24

ALL THINGS HAVE BEEN CREATED
THROUGH HIM AND FOR HIM.
HE IS BEFORE ALL THINGS,
AND IN HIM ALL THINGS HOLD TOGETHER.

Colossians 1:16–17 NIV

TODAY, I AM FINDING GOD'S STRENGTH IN

Weakness Is Spelled S-T-R-E-N-G-T-H

BY KATHI LIPP

Don't do it, Kathi, I hiss to myself in my brain. Still, I cannot help myself. I finish looking at each person in the space and come to the same conclusion almost every single time: I am the biggest girl in the room.

People who love me reassure me, "No one is thinking that! You're awesome!" And as much as they aren't thinking it (because they don't see that part of me first anymore), I have evidence that others do see it. I don't understand why this is an area I have wrestled with all my life. Why does my weakness need to be the first thing people see when I walk through the door?

If you, too, are one of the ________est women in a room, (fill in the blank), I get it. But I've realized that while people see my weakness first, weakness isn't always a bad thing. I can't tell you the number of times someone has said some variation of the following to me:

"I could tell you wouldn't judge me."

"I'm having a hard time, and I thought you would understand."

"I knew you would get it."

These people don't know a thing about me. Do I love my husband? Do I put my grocery cart away? How do I treat my dog? They don't know, but I've been given unearned access into hard places simply because of my BMI. People look to others to find safety in sharing their own pain. My weakness, to some people, is the shortcut to safety.

God can and will do powerful things through those of us who give our weakness over to Him because His glory shines brightest in weakness.

Do I want to stay stuck? Of course not. But just because I don't want to stay in my weakness doesn't mean God cannot—and will not—use it for His glory. You, too, can trust God to use your weakness to put His power on display.

Day 25

EACH TIME HE SAID, "MY GRACE IS ALL YOU NEED.
MY POWER WORKS BEST IN WEAKNESS."
SO NOW I AM GLAD TO BOAST ABOUT MY WEAKNESSES,
SO THAT THE POWER OF CHRIST CAN WORK THROUGH ME.

II Corinthians 12:9 NLT

TODAY, I AM FINDING GOD'S STRENGTH IN

Every Rejection Is an Invitation to Open Doors Meant for You

BY LUCRETIA BERRY

When I was a little girl, my dad shared some lifelong wisdom with me. He told me, "What is meant for you will be for you." As a child, my dad's wisdom softened the sting of all the rejections I would experience in life. I learned to see rejection as a force drawing me toward a space where I belonged. However, it's not easy to dust off disappointment and focus on an invitation to an unknown.

As I grew up and matured in my understanding of God, I realized that my dad's wisdom resonated with God's character. Essentially, it is because of who God is that I can confidently peer past disappointment to push toward discovering an opportunity that awaits me.

And what do I know about God? Through the Old Testament prophet Jeremiah, God revealed that the Israelites could trust He had a greater plan in place for them—even as they were in exile. Although their situation felt bleak, they could hold on to hope because God wanted them to flourish, not fail.

I have felt the devastation of rejection many times, but knowing God wants me to thrive, not die on the vine, inspired me to pick myself up and look for the promised plan.

I am extremely grateful that while I was young, my dad shared God's truths with me: *What is meant for me will be for me.* I don't have to worry about missing out on an opportunity or be anxious about someone taking something that "belongs" to me. I've learned to trust that God wants me to flourish and thrive; He protects the plans He has for me. Therefore, I don't have to take rejection personally. I simply get to rest in the hope that rejection invites me to a clearer, more focused direction toward that which has been designed and orchestrated specifically for me.

As you face rejections, closed doors, and "missed" opportunities, may you know that God has a plan for you, goes before you, and has your back.

Day 26

"FOR I KNOW THE PLANS I HAVE FOR YOU," DECLARES THE LORD, "PLANS TO PROSPER YOU AND NOT TO HARM YOU, PLANS TO GIVE YOU HOPE AND A FUTURE."

Jeremiah 29:11 NIV

TODAY, I AM FINDING GOD'S STRENGTH IN

Could Fear Be an Invitation to Trust?

BY ALIZA LATTA

Stress felt like it was seeping into every part of my life. I was overwhelmed and fearful about seemingly everything. I felt far from God and far from my friends.

Finally, one morning, I collapsed onto my favorite chair and earnestly prayed for wisdom, strength, and the capacity to continue. What struck me was that everything I was stressed over had once been an answer to prayer. My jobs, relationships, friendships, church—each one of them had been something I'd asked God for.

How could I have so much fear over the gifts God had given me?

I thought back to last year: I was afraid about a variety of different things then. And the year before that? More fear about other areas of my life. I considered the future: Might I have things to be fearful of next year or the following year or the year after that? Based on my track record, I think so. If there's always something to be fearful of, what could I do with my fear?

The gentle voice of Jesus spoke within me: *What if this fear is an invitation to trust Me?*

Jesus invites us to cast our cares—our worries, our burdens, our stress, our overwhelm, our fear—onto Him. Most of the time, I'd prefer to hold on to my fear. But the truth is, holding on to it only makes me more fearful.

Could fear really be an invitation to trust? Instead of falling for the idea that we need to muster up enough faith or grit our teeth to make our way through our fear, could we instead accept Jesus's kind and gentle invitation to trust Him with it?

I remained sitting in my chair, but I closed my eyes and lifted my hands. I listed everything I was afraid of and told Jesus I was giving all of them to Him.

The fear didn't pass, not fully. But I pray we'll remember that our fear is an invitation to trust . . . and through that trust awaits an even greater invitation to be brought into deeper union and intimacy with Jesus.

Day 27

WHEN I AM AFRAID, I PUT MY TRUST IN YOU.

Psalm 56:3 NIV

TODAY, I AM FINDING GOD'S STRENGTH IN

In Our Darkest Moments, God's Shalom Protects Us

BY MICHELLE AMI REYES

Some memories stay with you forever. I distinctly remember one winter break when I was fifteen years old. A blizzard was unleashing its fury over our small Minnesotan suburb. It was negative ten outside, and I could feel the chill seeping through the windows. I found myself huddled in a corner of my family's living room, knees to my chest, watching the snow fall. I looked up at the cloudy sky and began to pray, "God, I need your peace."

My prayer was born of loneliness. I was a tall, gangly Indian American girl living in a non-Indian community, and I had a hard time making friends. I wasn't invited to my classmates' skiing outings or the occasional hangouts with sledding and hot chocolate. I look back now as an adult woman and think, "No big deal. I didn't need to go to those parties." But as a teenage girl, I felt that isolation and social rejection keenly.

The more I think about that moment—huddled in the corner, praying—the more I realize, what I was really asking God for was His protection. Protection from the unkindness of cliques and the unwanted mental battles that come when you feel no one wants to be your friend. Protection from lashing out, from believing lies, or even from returning meanness in kind.

At the time, it was just a cry for help. But over the years I've learned that God's true peace, the shalom that He promises us, has a distinctly protective nature to it.

I love the word "guard" when Paul writes that God's peace *guards* us. It's a picture of God's shalom as a fortress keeping guard over our hearts and minds, protecting us from emotional, mental, and spiritual assaults. God might not take away the infertility or the sting of betrayal or the grief of losing a family member or financial troubles, but He promises that those who trust in Him will have an inner calm in the face of life's storms.

May each of us know and rest in the protection of God's shalom.

Day 28

AND THE PEACE OF GOD,
WHICH TRANSCENDS ALL UNDERSTANDING,
WILL GUARD YOUR HEARTS AND YOUR MINDS
IN CHRIST JESUS.

Philippians 4:7 NIV

TODAY, I AM FINDING GOD'S STRENGTH IN

When Healing Tarries

BY KARINA ALLEN

There is a growing number of my friends and loved ones who have been hit with chronic illness—everything from cancer and ALS to migraines and digestive struggles. I'm hard pressed to fight alongside each of them as they so graciously do for me.

The last few years, my knees have been hurting. They hurt when I walk, sit for long periods of time, or go up and down stairs. I attributed it to aging, but I was diagnosed with patella tendinitis last year. Then I was in a multivehicle car accident that led to some deep tissue muscle damage.

I've always tried to have compassion for my friends who suffer daily from chronic pain, but I could never fully relate. This last year has been eye-opening and humbling. I've prayed and prayed for healing. Healing has come, but it's only been a little taste of it.

Often, our healing—both spiritually and physically—is connected to community. I have laid hands and prayed for my friends who needed healing. Some were instantly cured. Some simply felt better. Others passed away and received healing in eternity. I have also been on the receiving side of prayer when I have needed healing. I've felt seen and loved and valued. That was when community truly became the family of God in my life.

Healing isn't just good for us—it shows God's glory. When we've received healing, we can walk in the authority we now have and encourage others with our story.

We can easily become discouraged when our healing tarries. It's okay to walk through disappointment. But let that disappointment lead you to deeper trust in the Bringer of Peace and the Body of Christ, who can have faith for you and believe when you can't.

Day 29

BUT HE WAS PIERCED FOR OUR TRANSGRESSIONS;
HE WAS CRUSHED FOR OUR INIQUITIES;
UPON HIM WAS THE CHASTISEMENT THAT BROUGHT US PEACE,
AND WITH HIS WOUNDS WE ARE HEALED.

Isaiah 53:5 ESV

TODAY, I AM FINDING GOD'S STRENGTH IN

Don't Force It

BY ANJULI PASCHALL

My son and I fight a lot. It's not easy to admit, but we see the world so differently. He is strong. I am not. He is outspoken. I am not. He is opinionated. I am opinionated. Since he came screaming out of me sixteen years ago, he's been a fighter. After all this time, I'm weary.

In my weariness, I get defensive. I get angry. I want to demand my voice be heard. I want to make him see my point of view and why it's right.

I tend to force things. I can be stubborn. I want what I want. I've spent a lot of my life "forcing" things. I've done this with jobs I wanted. I push and push and push because I'm afraid of not getting what I want. I've done this with things, opportunities, and people.

When I'm afraid, I force my way forward.

I'm reminded of so many figures in the Bible who forced things too. Sarah was afraid of not conceiving and forced her husband to sleep with her servant, Hagar. Moses used force, Judah used force, and Peter used force—all when they were faced with a fearful situation. But, when I react to my fear by forcing my way forward, I usually end up hurting myself or others.

Life doesn't have to be a battle. We don't have to fight to get ahead or fear falling behind. Instead, we can surrender. We can let go of life on our terms. As fear rises, we can refuse to put on our boxing gloves and instead lean on Jesus.

I usually deal with my fear by using my own strength. When I sense my soul tensing up for a fight, I've learned to listen to the invitation to relax. I can enter my fear with Jesus. Like a litany, I live these words: *soul, be still*.

Don't force the doors of opportunity to open. Don't force people to relate in ways that only work for you. Don't push to get your way. Trust that the Lord is always present and will always lead you to love and be loved.

Day 30

SURELY GOD IS MY SALVATION;
I WILL TRUST AND NOT BE AFRAID.

Isaiah 12:2 NIV

TODAY, I AM FINDING GOD'S STRENGTH IN

God Wants to Give You Rest

BY BECKY KEIFE

I wrenched myself from the comfort and warmth of my bed. *You need this. It's worth it*, I reasoned. I knew I needed more of Jesus than more sleep. I heated a cup of lemon tea and sat down at my kitchen desk. I reached for my Bible, but yesterday's to-do list caught my eye. So many boxes left unchecked with many more to add. Urgent tasks and ongoing responsibilities and so many people depending on me. I dropped my Bible and my head. It was just too much.

I should open my computer and start answering emails before the kids wake up. Lord knows I need every quiet minute I can get, I reasoned with myself. *That project isn't going to move forward alone, and that misunderstanding won't resolve itself. I'll never conquer this list if I don't start now.*

As I grabbed my list and pen, the morning light caught the corner of my eye. I glanced out the window to see dawn breaking. Then, my eye zeroed in on a small bird perched on the telephone wire. I leaned closer and recognized the slender needle beak of a hummingbird. I had never seen a hummingbird at rest before. Dashing to-and-fro, zigzagging with frenetic intensity, yes. But never still.

Most of my life I've lived like a hummingbird—body and mind flapping a mile a minute in an effort to do all the things with focus and speed. But in truth, I was tired. Bone-to-soul weary.

As I continued to gaze upon the tiny resting bird, a different voice filled my mind: *Daughter, even the most vivacious and productive creature was created to rest. Not just rest from striving, but rest in Me. I want to take care of you today. Let Me.*

I pushed aside my list and my laptop and bowed my head again. Not in defeat, but in gratitude for being seen.

God sees you, too, and He wants to take care of you.

Day 31

"LOOK AT THE BIRDS. THEY DON'T PLANT OR HARVEST OR STORE FOOD IN BARNS, FOR YOUR HEAVENLY FATHER FEEDS THEM. AND AREN'T YOU FAR MORE VALUABLE TO HIM THAN THEY ARE?"

Matthew 6:26 NLT

TODAY, I AM FINDING GOD'S STRENGTH IN

A Resting Place for the Broken

BY RACHEL MARIE KANG

I ran as fast and as far away as I could, grabbing my keys and bolting out the door. Tears streamed down my face while my lungs heaved emotional release—*inhale, exhale, inhale, exhale*.

With my hands on the steering wheel, I drew in one, long deep breath, bringing both my body and soul peace. I took the main road that leads to a pathway paved under a canopy of trees. Body heavy and burdened, I walked the trail and made my way to the boulder at the water's edge. Elongating my limbs, I climbed. Then, I slid down onto the boulder's wide, flat surface.

The sky above spun with the softest shade of blue, and the wind blew like a breath that calmed my broken spirit. Looking out at the lake, I listened to the leaves rustling and opened my audiobook app to listen to an Indigenous people's translation of Matthew 5:4–5 (a way of listening to the Word that connects deeply with part of my ethnic heritage). On the boulder, I felt the heat of the sun warm up my skin. I curled up my body and closed my eyes while the gospel played, telling me how Creator cares for the ones who cry trails of tears and how the earth can be a holding place for the ones who know sorrow and pain.

Heart wide open, I saw it as clear as day: I was welcomed in the middle of my breakdown and brokenness as I rested on the strength and comfort of that boulder that belonged to the Lord. Though my spirit reeled and raged with emotions, through nature I was reminded that the Lord is a refuge. With my attention on His creation, I saw that He alone is a resting place for the broken.

I don't remember what triggered my tears that day, but this I know: We are loved by the One who is ever-present and all-powerful. The One who cradles us with comfort, even as we crumble and cry.

Day 32

FROM THE ENDS OF THE EARTH I CALL TO YOU,
I CALL AS MY HEART GROWS FAINT;
LEAD ME TO THE ROCK THAT IS HIGHER THAN I.

Psalm 61:2 NIV

TODAY, I AM FINDING GOD'S STRENGTH IN

The Surprising Ways God Speaks

BY MARY CARVER

Some Sundays are a sobbing-in-the-back-row kind of day, and this was one of them. The pastor had played a clip from *The Chosen* (a drama series about the life of Christ), and I couldn't keep it together. After Jesus urged the disciples to throw their nets to the other side of the boat and try one more time, we watched as they scraped up just enough hope to obey and then beamed with joy and wonder at the hundreds of fish filling their nets.

I was desperate and broken that day, in the midst of a season watching my daughter suffer immense pain that was both undiagnosed and untreated. We'd spent months in doctors' offices and pharmacies and emergency rooms. I'd done everything I knew and even a few new things in desperation; nothing had worked. I didn't blame God, but I was starting to question whether or not He was with us or would ever help us.

The overwhelming emotion I felt that Sunday morning took me by surprise, though it shouldn't have. For decades God has spoken to me using pop culture as a conduit of His truths and hope, wisdom, and strength.

Even as a child, I remember telling my mom about the first song I'd heard on the radio the morning my granddad died. "Mom, I heard 'Lean on Me,' and maybe God's telling us to lean on Him or each other." I'm not sure it was much comfort to her, but God's unique kindness that day has stuck with me ever since.

God doesn't just speak on mountaintops or in burning bushes, through hymns or even quiet times spent in Scripture. If we pay attention, He'll give us exactly what we need, exactly where we are. He'll give us strength in the struggle in the most creative ways. From a sunrise to a word from a stranger, from an intense prayer time to a superhero's speech on the big screen, God is pursuing us and providing for us everywhere.

Day 33

"BUT THE HELPER, THE HOLY SPIRIT,
WHOM THE FATHER WILL SEND IN MY NAME,
HE WILL TEACH YOU ALL THINGS AND BRING TO YOUR
REMEMBRANCE ALL THAT I HAVE SAID TO YOU."

John 14:26 ESV

TODAY, I AM FINDING GOD'S STRENGTH IN

PAYING ATTENTION

Walking with Him

BY ANNA E. RENDELL

Walking. I started walking, slow and steady and short, and working my way up to faster and longer and still steady. It's great for my head and heart to be outside, lost in thought or music, talking to myself and God and the dog. I am not an exercise lover or workout queen. I'm a walker, up to about three pokey miles at a time.

The end of the day, the fleeting moments before darkness swallows the sky, have always been my favorite time to walk. Sometimes twilight shows up as an ombré of blues. Other times it's half a gentle rainbow. Yet other evenings it's a fiery display of blazing reds and yellows. I love it all.

The calm from the sky, the quiet of the ending day, and the peace of the coming night settle me from my frazzled head down to my toes. This time of day signifies the start of rest, and its beauty is no surprise, thanks to the One who paints it each evening.

Taking a few minutes to shut out the noise and walk to the end of my street or on a path near the lake, helps me to pay attention to the glory hiding in the ordinary, no matter what's waiting at home or on my phone or in my email. When I walk, I'm able to pay more attention to the people in my life, listening to them and truly seeing them for the gift that they are.

Sometimes the beauty of God is super easy to see. Other times it's more hidden and waiting to be found. Especially when I spend time in nature, it reminds me of the glory and hugeness of God. Seeing His creation strengthens my soul and helps me to handle the small annoyances of the day, puts big problems I'm wrestling with in perspective, and reminds me just Who holds it all together.

I hope today you were able to see a glimpse of God's glory. And if you didn't, there's still time tonight—just start walking.

Day 34

THE HEAVENS DECLARE THE GLORY OF GOD,
AND THE SKY ABOVE PROCLAIMS HIS HANDIWORK.

Psalm 19:1 ESV

TODAY, I AM FINDING GOD'S STRENGTH IN

Remember How the Story Ends

BY KAITLYN BOUCHILLON

Two friends recently began the first book in a series I've come to love, so I promptly started book one again, ready for a refresh. Line by line and page by page, a grand story was woven together, culminating in an ending that wasn't quite what one might expect and yet was absolutely as it should be. It was right and good and beautiful. At a particularly nerve-racking moment in the audiobook, I interrupted the narrator and reminded my racing heart, "It's going to be okay. You know how the story ends." And then I froze in wonder and relief, because even though it's true while rereading a fictional story, the deeper truth is that Scripture offers us the very same hope: the assurance that come what may, it's going to be okay.

We may not know what the next chapter will look like or how we're going to make it, but we can be confident that God will bring us through the fire and the flood. There will be twists and turns along the way, but the end has already been determined: God will walk us all the way home.

Even when the darkness surrounds and suffocates, God hasn't gone anywhere. Even when we cannot see a way, God will not turn away. He's trustworthy and true, and the One who is in control knows exactly how the story concludes. God gets the final word, and it's guaranteed to be good.

As one of the characters so perfectly says near the end of the series, when they've made it through the seemingly impossible, "Dawn has conquered dark since the Maker spoke the world. The night is deep, but light runs deeper."[1]

Our hope is secure. The promise is sure. The weary world has reason to rejoice, for the story is in good hands. Dawn is already on the way.

Everywhere we look, even in a fictional book, are reminders that we're going to be okay. We know how the story ends.

---

1 "The Warden and the Wolf King by Andrew Peterson, page 205"

Day 35

"LOOK! GOD'S DWELLING PLACE IS NOW AMONG THE PEOPLE, AND HE WILL DWELL WITH THEM. THEY WILL BE HIS PEOPLE, AND GOD HIMSELF WILL BE WITH THEM AND BE THEIR GOD."

Revelation 21:3 NIV

TODAY, I AM FINDING GOD'S STRENGTH IN

Finding God in the Pebbles in Our Lives

BY KAYLA CRAIG

We drove up the coast of Lake Superior, rolled up our jeans, and waded into the waves. We were embarking on a bit of an adventure "hunting agates"—a type of rock with beautiful bands that originally formed from volcanoes.

My family and I had no idea what we were doing, but nevertheless, we felt fantastic about our newfound skills. Only it turns out . . . we're miserable agate hunters. The whole lot of us. I had this grand idea that these weathered stones would contain something gorgeous inside—except the stones we picked were mostly just . . . rocks. I felt like Charlie Brown after he gets rocks when he goes trick-or-treating.

Maybe the lesson is to enjoy the moment and not the end result.

I've been trying to be more present in my reality, but sometimes it's difficult. How can I see God when I clean the bathroom *again*? When my child asks the same question for the fiftieth time? I can be so focused on what is to come that I miss the delight of being in God's presence now. Of seeing the image of God in my life, in my neighbor, in myself *now*.

I'm reminded of Elijah and his experience of hearing God. He expected to hear God in the crack of an earthquake, in the fire after the storm. But instead, God spoke to Elijah with a still, small voice. We often think of God speaking to us through something grand. Through beautiful, multicolored gemstones. But what if God is speaking to us through the plain, brown pebbles too?

I still have my little sandwich bag of gray and brown rocks. I keep it in my office close to my desk. And when I hold the smooth tiny stones in my hands, I remember that God was with me then, is with me now, and will be with me in the future.

We think we find God in the fancy agates, but maybe we find God in the simple moments as well. Immanuel, God with us.

Day 36

AFTER THE EARTHQUAKE A FIRE;
BUT THE LORD WAS NOT IN THE FIRE:
AND AFTER THE FIRE A STILL SMALL VOICE.

I Kings 19:12 KJV

TODAY, I AM FINDING GOD'S STRENGTH IN

Learning the Way of Wisdom by Paying Attention

BY GRACE P. CHO

Soon after we got married, my husband and I moved to Las Vegas. We planned to raise our children there, commit ourselves to the local church, the people, the city. We never dreamed that after seven years, we would pack up everything and leave.

The move didn't happen because of a rift in relationships or drama in the church or being let go from our jobs. It was the kind of change that required time, prayer, and wisdom to know it was the next right thing.

I used to ask God for direction and then expect an answer to be displayed in lightning bolts across the sky. I was willing to do whatever God wanted, as long as it was clear that it was His plan. I prayed continually, trying my best to follow where I thought He was leading, but I often wondered if I understood Him correctly.

When our Vegas chapter was ending, there weren't any big doors closing or great opportunities sprouting. Instead, it began with just a sliver of excitement after hearing what God was doing in Southern California. Then it was the little things—seeing my husband's grandparents age more quickly each time we visited, remembering his grandma's prayer that we'd move back to California, noticing the quiet confirmations God gave that this was the right thing.

Wisdom can be gained in many ways, including paying attention to God's movements in and around us. We don't need lightning-bolt messages written in the sky for us to follow His paths. In Christ, we have the Holy Spirit who guides us into all truth and shows us the way.

It took a whole year of paying attention to God's movements and listening to His Spirit for us to eventually move back to Southern California. And we were able to go with confidence, knowing that whatever we did, wherever we went, God would go ahead of us and be with us.

Day 37

"BUT WHEN HE, THE SPIRIT OF TRUTH, COMES,
HE WILL GUIDE YOU INTO ALL THE TRUTH.
HE WILL NOT SPEAK ON HIS OWN;
HE WILL SPEAK ONLY WHAT HE HEARS,
AND HE WILL TELL YOU WHAT IS YET TO COME."

John 16:13 NIV

TODAY, I AM FINDING GOD'S STRENGTH IN

How Much More Will God Care for You?

BY JAMI NATO

I was so excited about our backyard plans! But as soon as the landscape architect mentioned that a door would come out right on top of my precious peonies, I stopped listening. My peonies are my prized possessions; they represent God's provision in my life.

We would need to move them now or lose them forever. So I watched videos and even consulted a peony farmer. Then, grabbing a shovel, I stood over the peonies and prayed, *Lord, You know how I feel about these things. Please don't let me ruin them. Help me do this right.* It seemed like a really silly prayer, but I figured I needed all the help I could get.

As I separated the bushes with the sharp spade, I could feel it dig into some of the tuber roots, and I cringed. But I remembered what I'd heard in the video: "As you can see here, I cut into these roots. But don't stress over that! They will heal. They might not bloom this year, but that's because they're healing underground. And when you split them, they'll sprout even more blooms."

Incidentally, God has been dealing with me on some personal root issues. It's like He's resetting me. I can't figure it out, but it's just such a tender time. I don't know why He's choosing to do it now.

The peonies didn't know why I was moving them. They were growing and blooming, and here I came with a shovel. But they couldn't see that if I didn't move them, they would be trampled, dug up, and discarded. Moving the bushes now was out of love, not inattentiveness or disregard. It was because I cared for them and wanted to help them bloom even more fully later on.

In the same way, God compassionately guides us for our good—out of generosity, not punishment and anger. He's all-knowing and all-seeing. He desires to heal us at the roots so in due time, we can bloom more abundantly.

Day 38

“AND IF GOD CARES SO WONDERFULLY FOR FLOWERS THAT ARE HERE TODAY AND THROWN INTO THE FIRE TOMORROW, HE WILL CERTAINLY CARE FOR YOU. WHY DO YOU HAVE SO LITTLE FAITH?”

Luke 12:28 NLT

TODAY, I AM FINDING GOD’S STRENGTH IN

Look for the Evidence

BY ALIZA LATTA

I sat in my counselor's office. I had many things I wanted to talk about, but before I could bring up any of the topics I wanted to discuss, I heard myself saying, "I am afraid to date. I'm afraid I won't be safe. And I'm afraid I'll make bad decisions. I don't know how to look for someone good."

My counselor took out a piece of paper, scrawling a word in capital letters near the top. In large letters I saw the word *EVIDENCE*. She drew a line down the middle of the paper and held it up to me. "See this?"

I nodded.

She told me to look for evidence in a guy's life: how he talked to his friends, the music he listened to, how he spoke to a barista. She told me to pay attention to everything: "Be alert and look for the evidence. The evidence doesn't lie."

I took her wisdom to heart. And I've realized that looking for evidence isn't only wisdom for dating relationships—it's also a way to see God.

I think of her words: *be alert and look for the evidence.*

Am I alert when it comes to seeking God? Am I looking for evidence of His love? When I truly think about it, get my trusty notebook out, and jot down the signs of God's fingerprints, I am astounded by all the ways He shows me He loves me.

I see the love of God in the eyes of my nephew and niece. I see the love of God in the friendships He has given me. I see the love of God in the way He's redeeming some hard parts from my past.

Be alert and look for evidence of God's love. I think you'll be surprised by what you find. God's love is as close to you as the air you breathe. He delights in you and sings over you. Sometimes we just need a reminder to wake up and look.

Day 39

"THE LORD YOUR GOD IS WITH YOU,
THE MIGHTY WARRIOR WHO SAVES.
HE WILL TAKE GREAT DELIGHT IN YOU;
IN HIS LOVE HE WILL NO LONGER REBUKE YOU,
BUT WILL REJOICE OVER YOU WITH SINGING."

Zephaniah 3:17 NIV

TODAY, I AM FINDING GOD'S STRENGTH IN

Miracle Chickens and God's Presence

BY BECKY KEIFE

On a cool October night in 1986, my mom bolted upright from a dead sleep and peered out her bedroom window. She saw a fierce orange glow dancing on the neighbor's roof. *Fire!* Only, it wasn't our neighbor's property that was ablaze. It was ours.

The next day, after the fire had been extinguished, we carefully made our way to the corner of the yard to see what had become of our chickens. My mom scooped up one of the Road Island Red hens and began to stroke its auburn feathers.

"Is she . . . is she dead?" I asked.

Without saying a word, my mom continued to pet the hen. Moments later, the chicken started to cluck.

"No, she's not dead! I don't think any of them are dead. They're just in shock." One by one, she held and patted each beloved bird back to life.

Over the years, I've thought back to that scary night and how God saved our chickens. The heat and smoke should have snuffed out their lives. The fences revealed that the fire had licked its way around the entire perimeter of our yard. While the coop remained untouched, the chickens, were not unmarked by the trauma. They were like five feathered statues frozen in place. It wasn't until my mom came into their space and reassured them with her presence that they were able to re-engage with life. It's a story that mirrors our lives in many ways.

Have you ever felt spiritually stuck? Mentally or emotionally frozen, unable to move forward because of pain, grief, or trauma? I know I have. It's in those very seasons of turmoil and overwhelm when God's presence can help us find our way back to life.

God doesn't expect us to navigate our trauma or move forward in our weakness alone. He draws near to us. He isn't afraid of our brokenness, our messiness, or how stuck we may seem. He delights in picking us up and carrying us.

Day 40

HE TENDS HIS FLOCK LIKE A SHEPHERD:
HE GATHERS THE LAMBS IN HIS ARMS AND
CARRIES THEM CLOSE TO HIS HEART;
HE GENTLY LEADS THOSE THAT HAVE YOUNG.

Isaiah 40:11 NIV

TODAY, I AM FINDING GOD'S STRENGTH IN

This Is the Amount of Faith You Need

BY JENNIFER DUKES LEE

Many years ago, a friend gave me a heart-shaped necklace with a mustard seed tucked inside. The mustard seed was so small, you could barely see it. At the time, that's how my faith felt after emerging from a very long period of doubt. It wasn't just that I doubted God's goodness or His love. I doubted His actual *existence*.

I wasn't an unbeliever, exactly. I was, what I call, a "wanna-believer." I truly wanted to believe. But a bunch of intellectual obstacles stood between me and God. Apparently, being a "wanna-believer" was enough for God. He hasn't given up on me yet.

So the mustard seed has felt sacred.

In a culture that values strength and abundance, I think we underestimate what God can do with a little. But the Bible reminds us that smallness does not disqualify you. I'm learning that it's not the size of my faith that matters, it's the size of my God.

These days, I no longer doubt God's existence. But my doubt shows up in other ways. I doubt that God will come through when I need Him to. I doubt that He hears me. I doubt that His timing is good. I doubt that He'll be faithful.

Recently I found myself overwhelmed with a long list of demands—and my faith felt too mustard-seed-ish to push through. I told a friend I was struggling, then added, "But God hasn't failed me yet." Sometimes, a declaration of God's faithfulness in the past will propel you to make use of your mustard-seed faith today.

Friend, God won't fail you. When you get to thinking you're too small or weak for the big things ahead of you, *think again*. Look to the teeny mustard seed. Stick this seed in the ground, cover it with dirt, add water, and it will push against the earth with great strength. The seed defies all odds to muscle forth in bloom. That's the power of *God* in the seed. And that's the power of God *in you*.

Your faith might feel small today. But God says it's worth something. He says it can move mountains. Stand back and watch what He does.

Day 41

"IF YOU HAVE FAITH AS SMALL AS A MUSTARD SEED, YOU CAN SAY TO THIS MOUNTAIN, 'MOVE ...' AND IT WILL MOVE."

Matthew 17:20 NIV

TODAY, I AM FINDING GOD'S STRENGTH IN

If It's Gonna Get Done, God's Gonna Have to Do It

BY BARB ROOSE

"I can't take it anymore, God! Why aren't You helping me?"

What looked like the end of my faith came in the form of a denial from my insurance company. I had noticed some developmental delays in my child and had learned about a diagnostic test that would provide the information we needed. When the coverage denial came a few weeks later, I slumped on my kitchen floor. I was disappointed God didn't answer my prayer. I wondered if faith was even worth it.

Suddenly, I realized I'd been treating God like an employee in my problem-solving instead of letting Him lead. In my effort to control the situation, I lost sight of the power, character, and sovereignty of God.

On that day on my kitchen floor, I uttered a new prayer, "If it's gonna get done, then God, You're gonna have to do it."

Years later, I'd come to realize that this was my first intentional act of surrender. Surrender doesn't mean we're giving in to hopelessness or defeat. Rather, surrender is giving over what we can't control to God, who not only knows more than we do, but is also bigger than we are and actually has control.

A few minutes after praying my surrender prayer, my phone rang. It was the administrative assistant from my child's school saying, "We wanted to let you know that you don't need your insurance company to pay for your child's test. There's a fund at the school that pays for that kind of testing." I hung up the phone in shock and gratitude.

Not every prayer is answered so quickly or how we want. But, as I reflect on God's timing, I believe He was saying to me, "Barb, if it's gonna get done, *I'm* going to do it—and I don't need your help." God was bigger and more powerful than my biggest problem, and I could trust Him.

Surrender doesn't guarantee God will answer instantly, nor does it mean God will behave as you want. It does mean you can trust God to be faithful, loving, and gracious, no matter the outcome.

Day 42

THE MIND OF A PERSON PLANS HIS WAY,
BUT THE LORD DIRECTS HIS STEPS.

Proverbs 16:9 NASB

TODAY, I AM FINDING GOD'S STRENGTH IN

When You're Tired of Trying to Make Everything Work

BY HOLLEY GERTH

I'm sitting in a drive-through line pondering a situation I can't seem to control. My husband and I are on vacation in Colorado, but I've been vaguely distracted by a situation back home.

"I can't figure out how to resolve it," I tell my husband when he asks what I'm thinking. I've fixated on this problem for months, looked at it from every angle, broken it apart, and put it back together.

Even on vacation, my mind can't rest. I feel weary and tired of worrying, exhausted from carrying the weight of what I can't seem to make right. I pause and pray: *God, give me the wisdom to know what work is mine to do today. I release everything and everyone else to You.*

I feel a shift within my soul as soon as I finish. I thought I wanted a solution, but what I really needed was to surrender. Stop fighting what I can't change. Start focusing on my own life instead of what I can't fix. Release responsibility for other people and return to what God has asked of me.

The funny thing? The second I said "amen" the person I'd been struggling with sent me a text message. I'd been holding on so tight, and when I finally let go, it seemed to unlock something in a way beyond what my human mind is able to comprehend. Of course, I still want to try to take control again. The situation isn't fully resolved. I've had to pray the same little prayer many times.

After I say "amen" I ask myself, "What is my work to do right now?"

I clean up the kitchen, hug my husband, walk a few steps, or pull out my laptop. I don't always want to do this. Sometimes I'd much rather whine, pout, and try to take charge again. Surrender is often a process, not an event.

If you're worn out from trying to control something or someone, I'm inviting you to say this prayer and ask this question too. Today, let's do our work, and let God do His.

Day 43

"FOR MY THOUGHTS ARE NOT YOUR THOUGHTS, NOR ARE YOUR WAYS MY WAYS," SAYS THE LORD.

Isaiah 55:8 NKJV

TODAY, I AM FINDING GOD'S STRENGTH IN

Hope for the Exhausted Soul

BY BECKY KEIFE

After eight hours sleep, I feel like a wreck. Shadows of intense, oppressive dreams linger in the corners of my mind. I realize I'm covered in sweat—again (nobody told me about this part of womanly hormones). I spy a sliver of dusty blue sky out the window. Hope awaits me away from this mattress, but I just keep watching the numbers on my phone slowly change.

I eventually wrench myself from my cozy covers. The couch welcomes me and my favorite cup of lemon tea. I open my Bible and read, "Rest in God alone, my soul, for my hope comes from Him" (Psalm 62:5 CSB). I slowly exhale, not even realizing I was holding my breath. The psalm continues, "Trust in Him at all times, you people; pour out your hearts before Him. God is our refuge" (Psalm 62:8 CSB).

Trust in Him. I trust God, but His Spirit pricks my heart and asks, *Yes, but what else are you trusting?* The list comes quickly: My determination. Someone else's ability to change. Hope that I can turn things around. Just a little more sleep. Enough boxes checked off.

Trust in Him at all times. Not just when I'm healthy and my kids obey and I keep all the balls in the air. God invites me—us—to unconditional trust. When sleep eludes or exhausts us. When people let us down or break us open. When there's no friend to catch our tears or money in the bank. This is when we get to trust God.

Pour out your hearts before Him. Could this be the remedy I'm aching for? God works in our hearts when we take our worked-up souls and bear it all before Him. There's something sacred and purifying in the intentional unraveling of every knot and jumble. It's where God's compassionate hands meet us and take over the real work.

I push myself up off the couch, weak and weary. And it's okay. God will carry me in His loving arms—not minding my dried sweat. I can already feel my soul starting to rest. Can you feel it too?

Day 44

GOD HAS SPOKEN ONCE; I HAVE HEARD THIS TWICE:
STRENGTH BELONGS TO GOD,
AND FAITHFUL LOVE BELONGS TO YOU, LORD.

Psalm 62:11–12 CSB

TODAY, I AM FINDING GOD'S STRENGTH IN

God Shows Up in Every Moment and Says, "I'm In"

BY MELISSA ZALDIVAR

After months of loss and grief and job searching, I sat across from my counselor. Deep down what I wanted to do was get very angry with Jesus because I knew that He could make something happen. I was fed up and ready to give Him a piece of my mind.

"Okay. Here's what I need to know," I said to my therapist. "What do you tell couples when one of them just doesn't want to be all-in anymore?"

For the record, I am single and have never been married. But I see my relationship with Jesus as a bond that is taken more seriously than any other, so the concept makes sense in my head.

She was surprised at first, having a single woman ask for marriage advice. Then she said, "It's important to keep welcoming them in rather than pushing them away. Even when it feels uncomfortable or easier to just deal with it alone. We have to show up and say, 'I'm in.'"

All our relationships will be flawed in some way. Either the other person will let us down or hurt us, or we'll do that to them. We cannot pretend that relationships don't take work. While Jesus brings perfect love and kindness and mercy to the table, He's also doing it knowing we're broken humans who get fussy and frustrated. And here's the wild part: He willingly and with great fervor comes after us and delights in us. He shows up, moment after moment, ready to keep moving forward with us to the very end.

There are days I need to walk in faith that Jesus really is close and that He really works for my good. But when I reflect on how He has carried me and the ways His character reveals that He's actually here to stay, I am reminded that this whole faith thing isn't about having a perfect relationship. It's about living out a binding commitment that God joyfully enters into, not out of obligation, but because He really meant it when He said, "I'm in."

Day 45

FOR HIS LOVINGKINDNESS IS GREAT TOWARD US,
AND THE TRUTH OF THE LORD IS EVERLASTING.

Psalm 117:2 NASB1995

TODAY, I AM FINDING GOD'S STRENGTH IN

An Urgent Invitation to Rest

BY GRACE P. CHO

I watched the cursor blink in the same spot, telling me I was wasting my time. Stubbornly forcing myself to sit at my desk hadn't helped move the work along. Through the window, I heard the kids call me again to watch them do cartwheels on the front lawn. I wanted to relish the last days of summer with them, but I was being pulled by the stern demands of deadlines.

I clicked through the many open tabs on my computer to find something that would require minimal thinking, but every task and project were at the point where they needed my focused attention. I closed my eyes, closed the laptop, took some deep breaths, and surrendered.

I leaned back in my chair, resigned and frustrated at my inability to push through. But then I sensed a different pull in my heart—an urgent invitation to rest.

Up until now, rest seemed like a luxury I couldn't afford. I'd started to believe that the mark of a generous, loving person was to give until I had nothing left. It was an unhealthy belief that I had grown up with—that being like Jesus meant martyring ourselves at the altar of service to others.

But we aren't robots created for incessant work, nor are we the saviors of the world. Rest is essential. We must rest so we can keep going. We must rest because we have limits and because we can trust God with all that needs to get done.

The lie that I was only as valuable as what I produced enticed me to open my laptop again and keep pushing through, but I decided to heed the warning to rest. I walked outside into the sun's embrace and watched with delight as my kids showed off their cartwheel moves. I sat on the front step and felt my body exhale.

We aren't meant to carry the world on our own shoulders. God's inviting you to rest. Surrender, exhale, and let Him love you.

Day 46

IT IS USELESS FOR YOU TO WORK SO HARD FROM EARLY MORNING UNTIL LATE AT NIGHT, ANXIOUSLY WORKING FOR FOOD TO EAT; FOR GOD GIVES REST TO HIS LOVED ONES.

Psalm 127:2 NLT

TODAY, I AM FINDING GOD'S STRENGTH IN

The Greatest Ruining of My Life

BY JAMI NATO

When I discovered my husband was having an affair, my whole world fell apart. But this was when I finally understood the gospel deep in my bones. Before my husband even showed remorse, I felt like God was asking me to forgive him. A Scripture passage I had written several months before glared at me from my chalkboard: "*Be kind and compassionate to one another, forgiving each other, just as in Christ God forgave you*" (Ephesians 4:32 NIV).

While he was still engaging in wrongful behavior, God asked me to demonstrate the transformative power of God's love to my husband. I can't begin to tell you all the work God did while my husband and I were separated. It was like God kept the sun from setting just for my heart to supernaturally heal. I came out a forgiving machine, renewed, strong—I had been with God.

It needs to be said that forgiveness is an alone game, but reconciliation is a together game. I worked alone for a long time to get healthy and to believe God would take care of me and redeem my situation even though it might not mean staying married. I sat in the uncomfortable in-between and trusted God for the perfect timing.

One monotonously normal day when I was standing at the door with a baby on my hip, I saw my husband walking down the street after not speaking to him for several weeks. I couldn't believe my eyes.

"You're it for me. I don't deserve to have you back, but you're all I will pursue for the rest of my life. I will do whatever it takes to come home. If you can forgive me. If you're willing."

Our long healing journey has not been easy. But my marriage has been a tree producing a wonderful friendship with my husband, shade for those walking through marital hardship, two more children, and the most delightful fruit in my own heart. All because God let me walk through the most terrible and most gorgeous identity awakening of my life.

To Him be the glory.

Day 47

BUT GOD SHOWS HIS LOVE FOR US
IN THAT WHILE WE WERE STILL SINNERS,
CHRIST DIED FOR US.

Romans 5:8 ESV

TODAY, I AM FINDING GOD'S STRENGTH IN

Everywhere I Look Is a Mess

BY ANJULI PASCHALL

Everywhere I look is a mess. I can't look at my house because it is falling off a cliff. Dishes are mounted up to my chin, and laundry, like lava, is overflowing onto all the floors. I can't look inward because nothing is organized. My sadness is mixing with my anger, and my anxiety is taunting my peace. I am easily triggered. Happiness can only be found if I can escape my reality and my mess, but the mess is everywhere. It chases me when I am on social media, I see it at Target, and I feel it at school pick up. Everywhere I look, there it is.

But I can't stop the mess. I can't steamroll sickness, make my boy obey, force my son to talk, or give my toddler all the control. I can't make people do what I want them to do.

I can only do this: receive and release.

I can open my hands and accept that this very moment is out of my control. I don't have to push the mess back, but I trust God is using it to make sense of my soul. My mess can become a place where I choose to praise.

He is using all things to bring my heart back into the right focus. A clean house, healthy kids, returned text messages, and finished projects never clean up the mess inside of me. Never. Only Jesus cleans up the mess. He is the one who holds my broken-up, battered-down, and bleeding heart. The mess is a gift.

The mess we encounter in our lives is merely another invitation to receive His love and release our need to fix ourselves. Whatever feels tangled and messy and wildly beyond your control, it is not too much for God. Hear Jesus's gentle whisper, "You can give it all to me. I can hold it all, while I'm holding you."

So, today, I clear out my schedule, cancel appointments, and put my sweats back on. The mess piles up in my house, but God holds the mess in my heart.

CREATE IN ME A PURE HEART, O GOD,
AND RENEW A STEADFAST SPIRIT WITHIN ME.

Psalm 51:10 NIV

TODAY, I AM FINDING GOD'S STRENGTH IN

Indescribable Relief

BY DAWN CAMP

There was a time when I desperately wanted a baby, but it didn't seem financially feasible. Three years earlier, I'd miscarried our third child, and there'd been a vacant spot in my heart, waiting, ever since.

We had no money, no insurance, but we had a solid marriage and a rental-condo-turned-loving-home. Initially my husband, being the more practical one, said we should wait. But I couldn't see beyond my instinctual longing for a baby felt by countless women throughout time.

We struggled intellectually and spiritually; often those points of view conflicted. We believed children were a blessing, but the lack of money and insurance was hard to overlook, harder still to overcome. Being in sync was important to us. Honoring God was also. My husband and I talked, cried, and prayed a lot.

Our final answer was that we didn't have a final answer. We admitted to ourselves and to God that we were lost, clueless, didn't know what to do. And then we surrendered it all to Him. Every last bit. *God, we have no idea what's right, but You do, so please take this burden from us.* Letting go was an indescribable relief.

Before long we discovered our third baby was on the way. Nothing else had changed. Then suddenly, everything changed: an unclaimed lost-and-found at work put money in our pockets; a friend called and offered my husband a job with insurance; out-of-state relatives shared a disbursement from an injury settlement. We shrugged and lifted our hands in wonder as these and other blessings appeared.

We now have eight children, but I look back on that season of wrestling and realize I've never surrendered my will more fully to His nor seen the Lord's provision in my life more clearly. Where does your longing clash with your logic? Is God inviting you to surrender your all? When we put our future in God's faithful hands, we see His creativity in answering prayers and providing tangible reminders of His deep love, mercy, and kindness toward us.

Day 49

TRUST IN THE LORD WITH ALL YOUR HEART,
AND LEAN NOT ON YOUR OWN UNDERSTANDING;
IN ALL YOUR WAYS ACKNOWLEDGE HIM,
AND HE SHALL DIRECT YOUR PATHS.

Proverbs 3:5–6 NKJV

TODAY, I AM FINDING GOD'S STRENGTH IN

When Envy Slowly Rots Our Souls

BY ANJULI PASCHALL

Her text was in all caps: *I GOT MY DREAM JOB!* My gut twisted. I tossed my phone down and turned on the water in the shower. I hated feeling this way. I wanted to text back, *I am so happy for you!!!* I knew the right thing to say, but my heart felt the wrong thing. This feeling was so painfully familiar: envy.

For me, envy has always been a struggle. If I'm being honest, I don't want it gone. But it's also honest to admit that it's slowly rotting my soul.

The water ran hot over my body. I needed to be cleansed. I saw how much I had let envy tangle me up. I didn't want to just say the right thing to my friend. I wanted to *be* different. I let the water wash over me and wept. *Lord, have mercy*. It was sad to see how much I had let envy roam freely in my soul.

I'm often afraid to trust that God will meet me in the middle of my mess. It's hard to hold on to Jesus instead of my jealousy. But I believe there is a better way. God promises the way to freedom is through Jesus.

For today, and I pray for tomorrow, I'm putting my foot down. I'm closing the door to the unwanted, slithery creature called envy that so easily takes up space inside of me. For far too long I've put my hope in my ability to manage, maneuver, justify, tone down, and tame my tendency to resent or long for what someone else has. But that's not the life I want. It cripples and cuts me off from my true source of love. Love is always within reach, but the choice to stand up to my envious nature or nurse it is always mine.

These real questions remain for each of us: What kind of life do we want? Do we want freedom or a soul warped by envy?

I dried off and texted my dear friend back, *YOU DID IT! I'M SO HAPPY FOR YOU!* I said the right thing, and my heart began to feel the right way.

Day 50

DO NOT BE OVERCOME BY EVIL,
BUT OVERCOME EVIL WITH GOOD.

Romans 12:21 NIV

TODAY, I AM FINDING GOD'S STRENGTH IN

A SHIFT IN PERSPECTIVE

A New Way to See Broken Things

BY SIMI JOHN

As soon as we moved into our new house, we planned to plant a willow tree in the backyard. We watched her grow and celebrated as her leaves danced with the Oklahoma wind. I have many memories of my kids playing under our beautiful willow.

Then Oklahoma was hit by a severe ice storm. When the ice began melting, I was so relieved that all my willow's branches were intact. Eventually, she stood tall again, but she wasn't the same. Her branches were disoriented and misshapen. One branch stood tall in the middle like an elephant's trunk while the other branches were left weak after fighting the freeze. She was forever marked by that storm.

Whether physical (or emotional) scars from childhood trauma, a dent on the car from a wreck, or an empty chair at the dinner table due to loss, life has a way of marking us. These scars remind us of the pain we've endured, the regret or bitterness we still hold. But what if their reminder is also a good thing? A reminder that we were bent and brought low but didn't break. That we made it.

In Genesis 32, Jacob wrestled with God, resulting in Jacob being marked with a limp. Jacob had carried the scars of pain he'd endured at the hands of others, and he carried the burden of regret for mistakes he'd made. But that night as he wrestled with God, he was given a new name—Israel, which means prince. As uncomfortable as his limp probably was, it became part of his identity, reminding Israel and others of God's presence and faithfulness. It marked him.

Friend, what if we showed our scars to the world? What if the brokenness we bear isn't meant to be lived in regret but to serve as a reminder—not of our weakness but of the strength of God? I pray that today you will see a God whose love is so amazing that He intentionally chooses broken things to display His grace.

Day 51

AND WE KNOW THAT FOR THOSE WHO LOVE GOD
ALL THINGS WORK TOGETHER FOR GOOD,
FOR THOSE WHO ARE CALLED ACCORDING TO HIS PURPOSE.

Romans 8:28 ESV

TODAY, I AM FINDING GOD'S STRENGTH IN

A SHIFT IN PERSPECTIVE

Make Those Dental Appointments and Open That Bible

BY ANNA E. RENDELL

I hate going to the dentist. But one spring, I had a toothache, and it was no longer avoidable. As my kind dentist finished the assessment for repair, she gently suggested we schedule my next cleaning as I was still mouth-open in the chair.

No escaping this, I thought.

For the next three years, I trudged back for appointments, fillings, cleanings, and more. I was petrified of what they would find and have to fix. Years of neglect had eroded my enamel and my peace. But as I continued going in, I slowly started to gain confidence. Now—finally—on the other side of my treatment plan, I recently had my first ever cavity-free cleaning. My doctor said, "Keep doing what you're doing! Your hard work is really paying off, and we can see it!"

On the way home, I realized that sentence had stuck with me. The dentist could see the effects of my routines. Isn't this just like our life with God?

This summer my family experienced a devastating loss. It's been painful, to say the least. But through it all, I've been so thankful that our love for Jesus has never faltered. Accidentally-on-purpose, I've spent decades building up my God-muscles. Reading the Word and tucking away truths. Praying, and asking others to pray when my words are gone. Knowing it's okay to fall into Him and cry.

This summer felt like walking into the dentist's office and bearing the marks of great oral hygiene. Our habits were put to the test. Would we hold up, or would we crumble?

The work we do today to build up our hearts and relationship with Jesus—the worship, quiet times, Bible study, reading and praying and studying—is what lays our foundation for tomorrow, and every day after that.

So make those dental appointments and open that Bible. Brush and floss and lift your hands in praise. Mouthwash like your gums depend on it, and write out your prayers like it's going to make a difference.

Because it is. Every single act of pouring into a relationship with God matters.

Day 52

I HAVE HIDDEN YOUR WORD IN MY HEART,
THAT I MIGHT NOT SIN AGAINST YOU.

Psalm 119:11 NLT

TODAY, I AM FINDING GOD'S STRENGTH IN

A SHIFT IN PERSPECTIVE

What Happens When We Wait

BY ALIZA LATTA

I remember waiting for my mom to finish her chemotherapy treatment years ago. We'd counted down the weeks until she'd be done. My dad planted a tree so we could wait for it to blossom, the same way we were waiting and praying for my mom to get better. We waited for her to finish radiation, then surgery, then at last, she finished with her treatments. Now it's been almost a decade since she beat the cancer beast, and I hardly remember how hard those days were.

I've never been good at waiting. When I was a kid at an amusement park, I'd opt out of the most popular rides because they had the longest lines and I never wanted to wait. I never liked to wait for the best option if it took too long. I'd settle instead for an okay option because it came faster.

But what if God's best for us sometimes comes with a long line of waiting? Isaiah 40:31 says, "They who *wait for the Lord* shall renew their strength; they shall mount up with wings like eagles; they shall run and not be weary; they shall walk and not faint" (ESV emphasis mine).

What if, when I'm waiting for Jesus, He is actually making me stronger? What if, in the waiting rooms, God is renewing my strength?

What if—as I pray day after day, month after month, decade after decade—the Spirit is empowering me to move into deeper trust, to mount up like an eagle, to run and not grow weary, to walk and not get tired? Not on my own, but through Jesus. With Jesus. Because of Jesus.

There are so many questions I don't have the answers to. But I do know that when we trust in Jesus, when we wait on Him, when we follow His lead to surrender everything—our dreams, our finances, our jobs, our relationships—He gives us His strength.

Just like an eagle, we're empowered to walk, to run, to soar.

That's what happens when we wait.

Day 53

THOSE WHO HOPE IN THE LORD WILL RENEW THEIR STRENGTH. THEY WILL SOAR ON WINGS LIKE EAGLES; THEY WILL RUN AND NOT GROW WEARY, THEY WILL WALK AND NOT BE FAINT.

Isaiah 40:31 NIV

TODAY, I AM FINDING GOD'S STRENGTH IN

A SHIFT IN PERSPECTIVE

When You're Caught in a Tug of War

BY BARB ROOSE

I was craving chips and guacamole. But after watching the news about a recent mass shooting of thirteen people, including eleven African-Americans in a supermarket in Buffalo, New York, I couldn't bring myself to drive to the store. I couldn't ignore the anxiety caused by simply being Black.

After the initial shock and sadness, I reminded myself that Buffalo was hours away. Snatching up my keys, I turned to go through my front door. I took a few steps and stopped, unable to go any farther. The thumping of my heartbeat was deafening. I slumped in my chair, stuck, frustrated, confused.

How do we get unstuck from anxious thoughts even though there may be a real basis for our fear? In the Old Testament, David began as King Saul's favored warrior but soon had to run for his life because Saul wanted to kill him. David only wanted to honor God, fight for his king, and live with his family. No matter how simple David's desires, his reality was complicated. I love that David admits to being overwhelmed, which many of us can relate to.

Thankfully, no matter our problem or pain, God specializes in freeing His children. You may not be able to change your circumstances, but you don't have to be stuck in your suffering.

As the tug of war in my mind continued throughout the day, I kept inviting God in. It sounded a lot like: "God, I know that You'll move me through this. My fears are real, but I choose to give You the final say." I could feel God tugging me closer to Him.

David tackled his fear in a similar manner. He didn't receive an instant solution, but eventually, God worked through David's faith to pull him out of his stuck place, even though he was still physically living in a cave.

God will free us from our stuck places too. Anxious thoughts can cause tough tug-of-wars sometimes, but we always have God's power to pull us through.

Day 54

YOU ARE MY PLACE OF REFUGE.
YOU ARE ALL I REALLY WANT IN LIFE.

Psalm 142:5 NLT

TODAY, I AM FINDING GOD'S STRENGTH IN

A SHIFT IN PERSPECTIVE

For the Days You Don't Feel Good Enough

BY HOLLEY GERTH

I'm curled up on my couch, laptop in front of me, thoughts swirling in my mind. I click keys and spill out my thoughts, until I type one line that makes me pause . . .

Just because something I do could be better doesn't mean it's not good enough.

That might seem obvious, but in that moment, it felt revolutionary. I've belonged to the "try harder" tribe my whole life.

I place my fingers back on the keyboard and type one more statement . . .

Just because YOU could be better doesn't mean you're not good enough.

Grace means that in all our mess, we are still enough. Jesus went to the cross and rose from the dead so we could be holy and whole; and when He said, "It is finished," He also declared, "It is enough," over our humanness.

The enough-ness we long for can't be found in improving our performance or becoming a perfect person. It can only be received, not earned. Despite our best intentions, we will mess up. Even when we try our hardest, we will fall short. This is the frustration and limitation of being human. But it's not something we can fully fix; instead, it's a reality to embrace. Why? Because it shows us how much we need a Savior.

I stopped typing, feeling a weight lift from my heart. I went online and found an image of the word "enough." I set it as my desktop screensaver so I could see it over and over again.

We'll continue getting better at what we do, becoming better as we grow into the people God created us to be. This is the work of a lifetime God promises to complete the moment we step into His presence. But the incompleteness of that process now doesn't mean we're failing. It's so important for us to know this truth deep down.

Just because you could be better, doesn't mean you're not good enough. That's true today no matter what because of what Jesus has done.

Day 55

THEREFORE, IF ANYONE IS IN CHRIST,
HE IS A NEW CREATION; THE OLD HAS PASSED AWAY,
AND SEE, THE NEW HAS COME!

II Corinthians 5:17 CSB

TODAY, I AM FINDING GOD'S STRENGTH IN

A SHIFT IN PERSPECTIVE

Let's Move Away from Scarcity Mentality and Live Abundantly

BY KATHI LIPP

Growing up, things were good in our family—until they weren't. Because of those experiences, the fear of "not enough" is deep in my DNA, and it's something I battle daily.

Sometimes my fear comes out in expected ways—paying bills late because I don't want to let go of the money we have, putting off repairs, lacking in generosity.

Other times, fear comes out in weird ways—buying too much at the store because what if we don't have the money to buy what we need next week?

I battle a heart of scarcity, but I long for a heart of abundance. But how do we apply it in day-to-day life? I've found that the best remedy is prayer. Prayer usually results in one of the following:

1. God gives me what I need. If I look hard enough, I discover I already have what I need. God keeps showing up and showing off to say, "Hey, remember those birds of the field? I've got you too."

2. God gives me another idea. Sometimes I'll be convinced I need something specific, but oftentimes I come up with another idea, another substitution, another something. I may not have exactly what I want, but God gives me the creativity to come up with what I need.

3. I realize I didn't need it in the first place. I've omitted a spice from a recipe, left a color off a painting, or done without an accessory everyone else seems to be wearing. And you know what? The world—and I—marched on.

When fears about not having enough come up, spending time with God reminds me how rich I am in many areas.

To move from a scarcity mindset to a place of abundance, we need to get quiet enough to hear the truth of the still, small voice of Jesus whispering to our hearts, "I am enough."

Day 56

I KNOW HOW TO LIVE ON ALMOST NOTHING OR WITH EVERYTHING. I HAVE LEARNED THE SECRET OF LIVING IN EVERY SITUATION, WHETHER IT IS WITH A FULL STOMACH OR EMPTY, WITH PLENTY OR LITTLE. FOR I CAN DO EVERYTHING THROUGH CHRIST, WHO GIVES ME STRENGTH.

Philippians 4:12–13 NLT

TODAY, I AM FINDING GOD'S STRENGTH IN

A SHIFT IN PERSPECTIVE

When You Wonder if God Is Really with You

BY KAYLA CRAIG

I'm a thrifter, and I once came home with a 1960s telescope. I know nothing about astronomy, but I love stargazing. The new telescope came with a menagerie of lenses, which were confusing. But my family and I cobbled pieces together with a screwdriver and a prayer.

A lunar eclipse was coming, so we brought the vintage telescope outside. There it was: the moon, big and bold, a reminder that the One who hung the stars was keeping watch over us.

The telescope didn't help us see the moon like we expected. We squinted and adjusted the lenses, but what we saw was a bit . . . blurry. It was easier to see with our eyes.

God's ever-present grace is like the swirl of the galaxies around us. We may not be able to see it—or even fathom it—but it's with us.

Sometimes we just need a shift in perspective. We can focus so much on having the right set of circumstances (or right telescopes) that we miss the glory all around us.

How often have you fallen into that *if-then* thinking? Maybe you've found yourself thinking, "*If* I just read my Bible more, *then* maybe I would see God's presence in my life," or "*If* I just prayed more, *then* maybe my circumstances would be better."

While Scripture reading and prayer are essential practices, the Kingdom of God is all around you, forever, like the moon. The daylight might obscure the moon, but that doesn't mean the moon isn't there.

In the moments when you're most overwhelmed and wondering if God's goodness can really be trusted, look at the night sky. May the stars remind you that even when you feel most alone, God sees you. The Maker of the heavens and the earth calls *you* beloved. The presence of Christ says *you* are worth finding. The grace of God says the Maker of the stars delights in *you*.

Day 57

LIFT UP YOUR EYES AND LOOK TO THE HEAVENS: WHO CREATED ALL THESE? HE WHO BRINGS OUT THE STARRY HOST ONE BY ONE AND CALLS FORTH EACH OF THEM BY NAME. BECAUSE OF HIS GREAT POWER AND MIGHTY STRENGTH, NOT ONE OF THEM IS MISSING.

Isaiah 40:26 NIV

TODAY, I AM FINDING GOD'S STRENGTH IN

A SHIFT IN PERSPECTIVE

Why God Calls Our Trouble Light and Momentary

BY MICHELLE AMI REYES

I have Bible verses I don't like. That's not to say I don't believe them. The entirety of God's Word is active, alive, inspired, and for our good. I know that. But some of the things God says are hard pills to swallow.

One of the verses in Scripture that trips me up is II Corinthians 4:17. It states, "For our momentary light affliction is producing for us an absolutely incomparable eternal weight of glory" (CSB). I've never liked the fact that God tells us that our struggles are "momentary and light." I often think, *God, if You only knew what I've gone through, You wouldn't call it light.*

Have you ever felt that way?

I remember when my sister had double kidney failure and almost died. I was in college and could barely function. How could I focus on classes when my sister was fighting for her life in a hospital bed? Around that same time, some of my closest friendships fell apart. I felt alone, helpless, and unloved.

I remember listening to a sermon about II Corinthians 4:17, and I almost wanted to scream at the speaker. How dare he say that what I was going through was momentary? At that moment, I *felt* like I was being told that the pains in my life didn't mean anything.

We all struggle. Maybe it's with our mental health, failing bodies, losing loved ones, or being wounded by people in our inner circles. As I've gotten older and experienced more hardships, I've realized that this verse isn't about minimizing our sufferings at all. God isn't telling me that my struggles don't matter. He's giving me a promise that one day my pain will end. In fact, He's telling us that even the worst imaginable suffering on earth will be nothing compared to the "eternal weight of glory."

God's Word gives us proper perspective. When we experience unimaginable grief, our Abba Father lifts our chin so that we can look up, not out. He whispers in our ear, *Persevere, my child. I'm here. Something better is coming.*

Day 58

FOR OUR MOMENTARY LIGHT AFFLICTION
IS PRODUCING FOR US AN ABSOLUTELY INCOMPARABLE
ETERNAL WEIGHT OF GLORY.

II Corinthians 4:17 CSB

TODAY, I AM FINDING GOD'S STRENGTH IN

A SHIFT IN PERSPECTIVE

It's Just a Matter of Time

BY ANNA E. RENDELL

I sat in on a company-wide marketing presentation focused on trending "aesthetics" that our younger consumers are identifying. Some of the concepts and verbiage were new to me. Just as I was thinking I was simply not hip to the trends, the presenter mentioned one final aesthetic: *goblin mode*. This trend entails sweatpants and hoodies, embracing stretchy pants and yesterday's mascara.

I thought, *Now that's an aesthetic I can get behind.*

I'm the first to share my dust bunnies and takeout, owning burnout and survival mode, living on grace and caffeine. But man, does it feel like I've been stuck in goblin mode for a while now!

There's another trend floating around where you identify your "toxic trait." I've been left pondering my toxic traits, which I've realized include testing the limits of dry shampoo, putting leftovers in the fridge knowing I will never eat them, and thinking that whatever the situation is (good or bad) it will probably last forever.

Combine that last trait with the allure of goblin mode, and boom—that's where I found myself during that corporate presentation—feeling a little bit ashamed, thinking I'd probably be stuck in goblin mode forever.

But we are never stuck in just one place. We have a good God who loves us way too much to leave us mired or marooned. Scripture is full of people who felt stuck and the God who rescued them—often from themselves.

Maybe we aren't stuck where we are. Maybe we're just here for a bit of time.

I find so much hope and much-needed perspective from the writer of Ecclesiastes who assures us that life happens in seasons—that there is a time for everything. From tearing down and building up, to laughing and weeping, mourning and dancing, to being silent and speaking. Life is never just one trend or trait or thing. There is a time for everything. It's all in God's hands. *We* are in His hands.

Perhaps we won't go from goblin mode to the newest trend. But we're not stuck forever. It's always just a matter of time.

Day 59

THERE IS A TIME FOR EVERYTHING,
AND A SEASON FOR EVERY ACTIVITY UNDER THE HEAVENS.

Ecclesiastes 3:1 NIV

TODAY, I AM FINDING GOD'S STRENGTH IN

A SHIFT IN PERSPECTIVE

A Forgiveness Beyond Comprehension

BY DAWN CAMP

I used to keep a mental highlight reel of my worst offenses. At the end of even the best day, my brain could hit the replay button, and scenes of my wrongdoings would scroll across the screen of my mind. Although I confessed those sins to God and asked for His forgiveness, I couldn't seem to forgive myself. Then I heard something that shook me to the core: to confess a sin, repent, and then continue to ask God's forgiveness for it multiple times (when you aren't repeating the sin) is a form of pride.

Did I believe my sins were so enormous and unique that they were beyond His ability to forgive? Despite the magnitude of God's mercy and of the sins I know He'd forgiven, why did I act like He couldn't handle mine?

We see divine forgiveness in King David's story. He didn't recognize the scope of his sin until it was exposed to him by the prophet Nathan. David repented, then followed the Lord the rest of his days, serving and honoring Him. God is merciful and forgives even the biggest sins when we repent and follow Him.

David could have removed himself from the narrative and wallowed in his own guilt for the rest of his life. Instead, he confessed and repented before God and then led Israel as God's chosen king for forty years.

Once I recognized how prideful it was to believe God could forgive the sins of others but not mine, I've never looked at myself the same way. Our difficult experiences—both the failures and the grace that covers them—can deepen our capacity for empathy toward others. Our darkest trials can become our greatest testimonies.

God's grace and capacity for forgiveness are beyond comprehension. When we give in to guilt and focus too much on our role as the villain in our own life story, we forget that God is the Hero who has redeemed us. Let's remember that we're covered in grace. Let's live in the freedom of His forgiveness.

Day 60

IF WE CONFESS OUR SINS TO HIM,
HE IS FAITHFUL AND JUST TO FORGIVE US OUR SINS
AND TO CLEANSE US FROM ALL WICKEDNESS.

I John 1:9 NLT

TODAY, I AM FINDING GOD'S STRENGTH IN

Worshipping Through Grief

BY DORINA LAZO GILMORE-YOUNG

That day will be forever etched in my mind. More than a thousand people gathered in the church auditorium to honor my late husband, Ericlee. I kneeled in the front row with my mother-in-law, my three young daughters, and a cloud of witnesses behind us. We lifted our hands in surrender, and even though our hearts were breaking, we praised God.

Dear friends gathered to form a worship band that day. The vocalists became a choir of angels singing all around me, and the instrumentalists ushered me into God's throne room.

This was a moment I expected to be consumed with sadness, but I wasn't. The singing somehow lifted my soul and carried me through the memorial service, as did the dozens of people who told me story after story of how my husband had impacted their lives.

When Ericlee was first diagnosed with stage four cancer, I had to rethink the purpose of worship. I was reminded again and again that God calls us to worship not just during times of victory and celebration, but especially in our suffering and grief. Worship is the way we enter into His presence.

I am challenged by Job's response to his suffering. Job lost all his servants and livestock, and then a mighty wind swept over his home, killing all his sons and daughters. Job tore his robe in grief, but then he immediately fell to the ground in worship. This shows me that one way to endure pain and hard circumstances is to get into a posture of praise.

I took care of my husband for months as the cancer painfully spread throughout his body. Watching him suffer was torture. The main thing that brought me out of despair in that season was worship. Worship is what continues to give me, and my daughters, strength as we grieve. Whatever trial, loss, or grief you're facing today, God's presence is your source of true strength. Enter His presence through the gift of worship. He is so worthy of our praise.

Day 61

NAKED I CAME FROM MY MOTHER'S WOMB,
AND NAKED SHALL I RETURN. THE LORD GAVE,
AND THE LORD HAS TAKEN AWAY;
BLESSED BE THE NAME OF THE LORD.

Job 1:21 ESV

TODAY, I AM FINDING GOD'S STRENGTH IN

A Song for Help in Broken Places

BY TASHA JUN

My left hand is misshapen, twisted, and scraped. My fingers feel disconnected from the rest of my arm. I try to push my palm back into place. Pain sirens through my arm like a stern warning. I ask myself why I'm so clumsy, and I scold myself for being so upset when it could've been worse.

I stand on the sidewalk for a moment feeling foolish, hoping no one saw me fall. I decide to walk home, pushing my twisted bike frame, one slow step at a time.

As I stumble forward, I try to put words together to pray but can't. I sing instead.

In off-key whispers, I plead by song with the One who says His help is ever-present and not limited to cases bigger and seemingly worthier of need. I do what the song says and lift my eyes up from the crooked metal. My voice rises as I ask where my help comes from and agree that it comes from the Maker of heaven, the Creator of the earth—the One who is there with me.

After hand surgery, buttoning my pants, putting my thick hair into a ponytail, and opening my kids' water bottles stack up into a long list of things I can no longer do on my own. I wince as I try to move my stiff wrist and exercise the muscles like I've been told to. My son furrows his thick brows, asking me, "Why can't you move yet? Why does it have to hurt? And why did it happen at all?"

I tell him I don't know the answers to those questions but invite him to do the exercises with me. We laugh as we bend our fingers in tandem, carrying each other through the pain of what we don't understand. We surrender to the mystery of song and joy that still rises from broken things, and I remind him that we have an ever-present Help who will not be thwarted from making all things new.

Day 62

I LIFT UP MY EYES TO THE MOUNTAINS—
WHERE DOES MY HELP COME FROM?
MY HELP COMES FROM THE LORD,
THE MAKER OF HEAVEN AND EARTH.

Psalm 121:1–2 NIV

TODAY, I AM FINDING GOD'S STRENGTH IN

POWERFUL PRAISE

Fear Won't Have the Last Word

BY BECKY KEIFE

The morning after I had hip surgery, I grabbed my phone to answer a text. But I couldn't read the screen. I was about to ask my son to bring me my glasses when I realized I was *wearing* them. Something was wrong. Turns out, I was suffering from an anesthesia side effect. My ability to calibrate between seeing near and far was seriously off.

As each day passed, I got more behind on work and more anxious. My doctor said the issue should resolve in a few days. But after six days of a massive headache and nonstop nausea, on top of regular surgical recovery, I was feeling severely discouraged.

The next morning my husband asked if I felt up for going to church. "No . . . but I want to go anyway."

My heart needed to worship. I needed to stop thinking about what was out of whack with my body and start focusing on what was right and steady with God.

As soon as the first song started to play, a lump rose in my throat. A lump of weariness for the long road of injury and healing. A lump of gratitude for all the ways friends and family had stepped in to care for me and my guys. A lump of tension because it's hard to be a doer sidelined from doing.

When my leg started to ache, I sat down, closed my eyes, opened my hands. As the worship team sang about Jesus silencing fear, tears slid down my cheeks, and I prayed.

Jesus, I'm afraid my vision is going to be permanently altered. I'm afraid this headache and dizziness will prevent me from doing my job. I'm afraid I'm failing. Jesus, I'm afraid, but I trust You. I surrender these fears to You. I don't want them anymore.

In my mind, I saw Jesus's hands wrapping around each fear. My eyes were still closed, but I felt the light rushing in.

The song ended, and I clicked on the Bible app on my phone to read along with the passage. Then I realized I was reading along! I looked around the sanctuary, and I could see! Now the only thing blurring my eyes were tears of awe and gratitude.

Friend, I don't know why God brings physical healing to some and not to others. But I do know this: Jesus is greater than the fear and darkness. You don't have to carry your burdens and fears alone. Jesus is with you.

Day 63

"DON'T BE AFRAID, FOR I AM WITH YOU.
DON'T BE DISCOURAGED, FOR I AM YOUR GOD.
I WILL STRENGTHEN YOU AND HELP YOU.
I WILL HOLD YOU UP WITH MY VICTORIOUS RIGHT HAND."

Isaiah 41:10 NLT

TODAY, I AM FINDING GOD'S STRENGTH IN

The Gift of Daily Graces

BY DAWN CAMP

"It seems like everything is going wrong," my husband said, discouragement evident in his tone and written on his face. The fan in one of our AC units stopped spinning, and the wall in my son's room was so hot the outlet cover had begun to discolor. Before that it was our dishwasher that suddenly quit filling with water, and the washing machine still had a leak.

Though my husband always manages to fix our household issues, the truth is that things fall apart.

I often look to the future for something big I want to happen or hope to achieve. But in weeks when everything's falling apart, I remember the greatest comfort can be found in such simple things: the touch of cool sheets as I crawl into bed, sleeping through the night in safety, ice for my water, curling under a blanket with a bowl of buttered popcorn and a movie on a Friday night, snuggling with a sleeping baby, ice cream for dessert.

Perception influences what we make of life: *Do I appreciate what's in front of me every day or only after I lose and regain it, like my air conditioning or my dishwasher?*

Sometimes we get caught up with life and miss the daily graces that surround us. It's easy to take the everydayness for granted and overlook the blessings in it. What might it look like to search for simple, largely unnoticed gifts? Point them out to the people around you, and let's thank God together for what He's done.

Praise God when your people make it home safely at the end of the day. Praise God when hot water comes out of your pipes and cold air from your vents. Praise God for the ability to clean your clothes and wash your dishes. And when everything seems to go wrong? Praise God anyway because He is good, all the time, and stands beside you through the good and the bad, through it all.

Day 64

I WILL GIVE THANKS AND PRAISE THE LORD,
WITH ALL MY HEART; I WILL TELL ALOUD
ALL YOUR WONDERS AND MARVELOUS DEEDS.

Psalm 9:1 AMP

TODAY, I AM FINDING GOD'S STRENGTH IN

I Am Who God Says I Am

BY MICHELLE AMI REYES

The light turned yellow, then red, and I slowed my car to a stop at the stoplight. *You're a failure.* The thought flashed across my mind, suddenly, unexpectedly. *Whoa, where did that come from?*

In the span of about three seconds, I began a battle of wits with myself. Half of me was chucking names like grenades—*unloved, unwanted, unworthy*. Memories of failed relationships and mistakes I've made flooded every corner of my mind. The other half of me was struggling to fight back—*no, don't think that. You know that's not true*.

The light turned green, and suddenly I felt exhausted—mentally, spiritually, emotionally. I was on my way to an appointment, but my confidence had just been stripped away.

Perhaps providentially the radio was playing the song, "I Am Who You Say I Am." Instinctively I tapped along to the tune. It was a song I'd sung many times before, and the last thing I expected was to be brought to tears by the chorus. I thanked God for reminding me that I'm not forsaken and He is for me—that I am who *He* says I am.

In that moment, I realized that the only opinion that truly mattered about me was God's. Not my own worst thoughts about myself. Not the words of people who don't like me or who see me in the worst possible light. Humans' words are fickle, but God's words are always true. I am who God says I am, and so are you. He calls us chosen, beautifully and wonderfully made, beloved, and His child. Nothing about us is truer than how much God loves us and delights in us.

Ever since that day in the car, I've found myself repeating to myself quite often, "I am who *You* say I am." We can't always change people's opinions of us, but we can trust that God's opinion of us is good and perfect and worth believing.

Day 65

I WILL GIVE THANKS AND PRAISE TO YOU,
FOR I AM FEARFULLY AND WONDERFULLY MADE;
WONDERFUL ARE YOUR WORKS,
AND MY SOUL KNOWS IT VERY WELL.

Psalm 139:14 AMP

TODAY, I AM FINDING GOD'S STRENGTH IN

And Even If He Does Not

BY MICHELE CUSHATT

Why does God deliver some miracles and seemingly withhold others?

I've been fighting cancer on and off for thirteen years now. This is my longest stretch without a recurrence, and for that I'm thankful. But I live with the pain and disability of a body that's been ravaged by disease and the treatments to overcome it. Some days I question even while I give thanks: *Why the many years of suffering?*

I find great comfort in an old story of three men in the book of Daniel. Faced with being burned alive in a furnace for refusing to worship false gods and a pagan king, Shadrach, Meshach, and Abednego had to choose: denounce their confidence in the one true God or believe Him one more time. They declared, *Our God is able, and He will deliver . . . But even if He does not. . . .*

Hidden in these two phrases is my secret for making peace with the prayers that are answered and those that are not. I don't doubt God's ability. He can make tumors disappear, bring prodigals home, heal marriages that are broken. He can make a way where there is no way, and He has done so more times than you and I know.

But even if He does not, He is still worthy of my worship. I trust Him in the healing and in the absence of it. I trust Him in the answers and in the questions.

Why? Because I need *Him* more than I need *healing*. The object of my affection and worship isn't this body, this life. It's the face of the One who saved me.

Keep praying, my friends. Keep asking, seeking, knocking, and believing with great boldness and confidence. Our God is able to deliver you. But even if He does not, remember: what you and I need most is not the thing we're praying for but the One we're praying to.

Day 66

[GOD] WILL DELIVER US FROM YOUR MAJESTY'S HAND. BUT EVEN IF HE DOES NOT, WE WANT YOU TO KNOW, YOUR MAJESTY, THAT WE WILL NOT SERVE YOUR GODS OR WORSHIP THE IMAGE OF GOLD YOU HAVE SET UP.

Daniel 3:17–18 NIV

TODAY, I AM FINDING GOD'S STRENGTH IN

When the Noise of the World Is Overwhelming

BY BECKY KEIFE

I live in a Los Angeles suburb with a small-town feel. You can't enjoy a latte at Classic Coffee without seeing someone you know. But for all the quaint charm, I often feel achingly overwhelmed.

Life presses from all sides. I can't seem to keep track of Little League schedules or who to drop off where or when. I run to Walmart and remind myself to breathe in the congested aisles when florescent lights flicker and I start to feel drifty and can't remember what's on my list.

I live a beautiful, ordinary, busy life, but it sometimes leaves me feeling wrung out. I'm a sensitive person, and the incessant lights and noise and hustle make my soul weary. I struggle to stay connected to God and others when all I want to do is retreat into a quiet cocoon.

And God isn't surprised. Instead, He invites me away. He beckons me to the trail. Just five minutes from our house sits a beautiful canyon. Tall pines, oaks with twisted branches, and lush ferns line the trail. I let my husband and sons walk ahead. I enjoy their laughter and banter. Then I block it out and listen to the insects I can't see and the rustle of the breeze playing in the trees.

Here I don't have to remember to breathe. I don't have to check anything off a list or battle the busyness. Here I feel close to God. Praise and prayer pour out of my soul as my feet pad the trail. I remember that my weariness is welcomed and the God of the canyon is also Lord of my life.

When life is too loud or too rushed . . . when you feel surrounded but all alone . . . God knows. He invites you to breathe. On a park bench, a sandy shore, or a shady trail, find a way to spend a little time in the beauty He made. Surely, you'll find yourself praising His name.

Day 67

SING A NEW SONG TO THE LORD!
LET THE WHOLE EARTH SING TO THE LORD!
SING TO THE LORD; PRAISE HIS NAME.
EACH DAY PROCLAIM THE GOOD NEWS THAT HE SAVES.

Psalm 96:1–2 NLT

TODAY, I AM FINDING GOD'S STRENGTH IN

POWERFUL PRAISE

Praising in the Heartbreak

BY ALIZA LATTA

I sat on my bed, rocking myself in the fetal position. Tears poured down my cheeks. A romantic relationship had ended abruptly just days earlier. My heart felt like it had been shattered into a thousand pieces. Every sad love song that had ever been written felt true.

I didn't want to work; I didn't want to speak to anyone; I didn't want to put on makeup or go to meetings or meet my deadlines. I wanted my life to go back to the way it was just a handful of days earlier—before it felt like everything had imploded.

I reached for my phone. I planned to play songs about heartbreak and devastation; I planned to throw myself a pity party. Instead, I found myself turning on worship music. Then I found myself praising God *before* my breakthrough—*before* the answer—because I trust in Him.

The worship song played loudly in my bedroom on repeat. I sang the words, over and over. I sang until my voice gave out, breaking. I sang until the tears dripped down my face and my vision blurred.

There was no way to know if my relationship would be pieced back together or if the prayers I cried out at three in the morning would be answered the way I wanted. I had no idea if the future I pictured would come to pass, or if I'd see redemption from my heartbreak any time soon. But I wanted the words I sang to be true. I wanted to sing, not because I knew everything would work out, but because I trusted in Jesus.

We aren't promised a pain-free life. We aren't promised every answer. But because we trust in Jesus, we can praise Him in the heartbreak.

In the middle of our heartbreak, we don't feel like we know very much. Everything feels uncertain and shaky. But we do know Jesus: Jesus, who never changes. Jesus, who remains constant and steady. Jesus, who is our ever-present help in times of need.

Even in heartbreak, we can trust in Him, and we can praise Him.

Day 68

I WILL PRAISE THE LORD AT ALL TIMES.
I WILL CONSTANTLY SPEAK HIS PRAISES.

Psalm 34:1 NLT

TODAY, I AM FINDING GOD'S STRENGTH IN

When the World Feels Like Too Much

BY ROBIN DANCE

What are we to do when our world no longer makes sense? What are those who follow Jesus to do? I believe an old refrain holds the key:

Turn your eyes upon Jesus, Look full in His wonderful face,

And the things of earth will grow strangely dim, In the light of His glory and grace.

A while back, I had the sweet privilege of serving women in my area as a leader for a community Bible study. Before we'd meet every Thursday, our leadership team began by singing this familiar chorus.

Tendering our hearts in song was effective. The things of earth—never-ending to-do lists, work deadlines, disagreements among friends, challenges with children, arguments with a spouse, health concerns, financial pressures, the clatter of politics, even some of our anxieties and feeling not enough—grow strangely dim. Our worries wither under the blaze of God's glory. When we focus on Jesus instead of circumstances, our circumstances may not change, but we sure do.

I know what it's like to wander around and feel lost, to wrestle in a sea of doubt, to question beliefs you once held dear. And while I don't know what's going on with you personally, I know all of us are affected by what's going on in the world.

How can we possibly handle it? We can't. We aren't even supposed to—that's why we have a Savior! Isn't that liberating?

Let's remind one another that the gospel is *good* news. When we are mindful of who God is and what He has accomplished in our lives and in our world; when we trust that He is good and loves us without condition; when we study His Word, claim His promises, and accept the forgiveness He offers; when we believe that He holds the whole world in His hands; when we turn our eyes upon Jesus, we *will* find peace.

To me, focusing on Jesus isn't just one way we can best handle a world that feels crazy. It's the only way.

Day 69

I LIFT UP MY EYES TO YOU,
TO YOU WHO SIT ENTHRONED IN HEAVEN.

Psalm 123:1 NIV

TODAY, I AM FINDING GOD'S STRENGTH IN

A New Song of Praise

BY KARINA ALLEN

The struggle is real. How do I know? I struggle. Struggle seems to find me wherever I go. I can't escape it, and neither can you.

It's not the most encouraging thing I could say, but that's life. And it's okay. Jesus never promised that this life would be without struggle. But He did assure us that He would overcome it all.

He overcame it in more ways than I can imagine. That should bring me comfort when I remember. And it does . . . *when* I remember. But the problem is . . . I forget. We all are prone to suffer from spiritual amnesia.

A new situation or new trial comes, and I forget the Lord's past faithfulness. I forget about His provision, or His support. I forget about all of His miracles in my life. I don't do it on purpose. I hate that I do it at all. But it does happen—more often than I care to admit.

At this moment, I'm in the middle of another difficulty. It's hard. It's completely out of my control. There is nothing I can do to fix it. But I'm grateful that I know the One who can, the One who has everything under His control.

The Lord reminded me of Psalm 96. The writer declares how good and holy and great God is. He is Creator and Sustainer. His name is above all names. He is full of splendor and majesty, strength, and beauty.

We are prompted to praise and worship, to ascribe, or acknowledge to the Lord that we know the glory of His name. When I view God rightly, my perspective changes. I no longer view my circumstances as overwhelming. I don't have to come up with a solution. I get to rest in His love and trust His purposes and timing for my life.

Highs and lows will come, but God is guaranteed to be greater. So let's sing a new song of praise to God over whatever situation we face today. May we bless His name and declare His glory.

Day 70

ASCRIBE TO THE LORD THE GLORY OF HIS NAME;
BRING AN OFFERING AND COME BEFORE HIM.
WORSHIP THE LORD IN THE SPLENDOR OF HIS HOLINESS.

I Chronicles 16:29 CSB

TODAY, I AM FINDING GOD'S STRENGTH IN

VULNERABLE CONNECTION

Bringing Light into Our Lonely Silos

BY MELISSA ZALDIVAR

I haven't said a word in hours. As a single woman, I spend a lot of my time alone.

The Bible is full of people who encountered Jesus from all walks of life. They were single, married, betrothed, working, impoverished, wounded, and strong. And when the church is established in the book of Acts, we're told over and over again that they gathered together and supported one another.

The church is the gathering of God's people, and our faith in Christ causes us to have "all things in common." Is this easy? Heck no. But when we're willing to be inconvenienced to live out the vision of Acts, the kingdom is built.

So am I willing to get interrupted by a toddler who got out of bed again so I can still connect with a friend who must stay home after 8 p.m.? Is it possible for me to attend a wedding and rejoice rather than retreat into self-pity? Will I understand Jesus's love better by surrounding myself with children, watching them live with wonder and simple faith? The answer to all these things is a resounding yes because God made us for community.

We often don't get close to one another out of suspicion and division, but we're called to break bread together—with gratitude! Moms and wives and students and single gals are all struggling with mostly the same things: not knowing what's for dinner, how not enough dresses have pockets, how not enough grocery stores carry our favorites. No one has consistent cell phone coverage. No one is reading their Bible without putting forth some effort.

Let's bring light into the loneliness of being in our silos. Let's be willing to be inconvenienced for the sake of community.

So send a text. Meet the person you don't believe you have common ground with. I guarantee you're both tired and hungry and looking for Jesus. And honestly? That's usually the best place to start.

Day 71

ALL THE BELIEVERS WERE TOGETHER AND HAD EVERYTHING IN COMMON. . . . THEY BROKE BREAD IN THEIR HOMES AND ATE TOGETHER WITH GLAD AND SINCERE HEARTS, PRAISING GOD AND ENJOYING THE FAVOR OF ALL THE PEOPLE.

Acts 2:44, 46–47 NIV

TODAY, I AM FINDING GOD'S STRENGTH IN

VULNERABLE CONNECTION

Inappropriate Laughter and Being in It Together

BY KATHI LIPP

I click on the link in our group chat and cackle so loud I scare the dog. My husband, Roger, from across the room, says, "Who sent you something inappropriate?"

"Michele," I answer.

"Figures."

Roger knows. Because Roger knows me and the "Bad Moms." The Bad Moms is a small group of friends who all have adult kids and who have all been told, at one time or another, that we were Bad Moms. (By those kids. Or ourselves. Or both.) We now wear that title as a badge of honor because we've all had to disappoint our kids in order to be the best kind of moms we know how to be.

We are the mom friends who send each other funny videos and inappropriate memes because let's face it: parenting doesn't stop when the kids move out. And these kids? They will make you cry. But the right kind of friends will make you laugh.

These are the send-money-for-a-dozen-donuts friends. The love-each-other's-children friends. They also lament when one of those kids is driving a fellow mom to eat every one of those donuts. And the way we have been bonded together? Disappointment. Grief. Pain.

There are a million Facebook groups, TikTok videos, and books created to support moms with kids at home. But for moms of adults, this is my best support group. Our group shares more than its fair share of deep joy and inappropriate laughter.

There have been so many times I've prayed that God would take a burden away. Gratefully, instead, God has chosen to surround me with friends—real, authentic friends who will carry that burden with me.

Is there someone in your life who needs help carrying a burden? Or maybe they just need someone to offer the gift of inappropriate laughter and brevity in a world where it's so easy to feel heavy. Either way, it is through our shared sorrows and joy that we can make it through.

Day 72

CARRY ONE ANOTHER'S BURDENS;
IN THIS WAY YOU WILL FULFILL THE LAW OF CHRIST.

Galatians 6:2 CSB

TODAY, I AM FINDING GOD'S STRENGTH IN

VULNERABLE CONNECTION

For the Ones Who Feel All Alone in the World

BY ROBIN DANCE

Starting over in a new place, I braced myself for a season of loneliness. Community was elusive in our previous hometown—years marked by relational void. I had even grasped for friendships online, but those didn't translate well to real life.

At midlife, I wondered if it was possible to find meaningful friendship again. My "friendship desert" and hurtful rejections had left me wanting, wounded, and wary.

I prayed, drawing courage and strength from God. Still, it was unexpected when four strangers entered my life through a remarkable chain of events, women who also had been praying for accountability. I hastily named our meetings "GIFT: Girls In Fellowship Together." I soon realized the name was divinely inspired; these women were a God-gift.

Although we quickly connected, we didn't yet *know* each other. That would take intention and prioritizing time. So, we met, prayed often, and shared what God was teaching us. We celebrated life's joys—answered prayers, birthdays, our children's accomplishments. We braved life's trials—illness, death of parents, teenage angst, prodigal children, job insecurity and loss, marital challenges, family dysfunction.

We spoke hard truths and guarded each other's longings, brokenness, and ugliest parts. Centering on Jesus and logging hours together helped us build trust.

It's helpful to remember that the God who works all things together for good (Romans 8:28) already knows our wants, wounds, and wariness. He'll strengthen and draw us closer as we seek Him. This kind of intimacy with Jesus teaches us to be a better friend. I think void and rejection have helped me be a better friend too. How precious for our struggles to be redeemed by His purposes!

Are you currently in a friendship desert or afraid to let people in? Are you wanting, wounded, or wary? *Oh, friend* . . . you are not alone! Friendship can feel risky, but don't give up. Friends can remind you who you are and Whose you are.

Day 73

AND LET US CONSIDER HOW TO STIR UP ONE ANOTHER TO LOVE AND GOOD WORKS, NOT NEGLECTING TO MEET TOGETHER, AS IS THE HABIT OF SOME, BUT ENCOURAGING ONE ANOTHER.

Hebrews 10:24–25 ESV

TODAY, I AM FINDING GOD'S STRENGTH IN

VULNERABLE CONNECTION

We Can Bear Witness to the Glory of God in Each Other

BY DORINA LAZO GILMORE-YOUNG

I often find myself thinking about Mary, the mother of Jesus. This teenage girl was to be a womb for God, the mother of His one and only Son. I imagine she trembled when the angel revealed that her body would embody God Himself.

After Mary's encounter with the angel, she hustled to visit her older cousin Elizabeth, who was also pregnant as an angel predicted. (I like to call her Aunt Lizzie.) Aunt Lizzie was pregnant with John the Baptist, the cousin and forerunner of the Messiah in Mary's womb. Aunt Lizzie was in her third trimester, and Mary was in her first. When the two women were united, the baby leapt inside Aunt Lizzie's womb, and she was filled with the Holy Spirit.

These two cousins needed each other. Mary needed Aunt Lizzie to provide confirmation, affirmation, and encouragement to her. She was to be the home for God wrapped in flesh. Quite a job description for a teenager. Aunt Lizzie needed Mary who would labor for her long-awaited Savior. She also needed a friend through her geriatric pregnancy, someone to celebrate and anticipate this long-awaited birth.

Sometimes it takes another woman to help ground us and remind us of our God-given callings. These two chosen women—one older with wrinkles dancing across her cheeks, the other younger with eyes full of hope—were able to bear witness to His glory in each other. This is how God designed us all. We were not made to weather life's storms or taste sweet victories alone.

Perhaps you are hurting today. Perhaps you are lonely and wondering if you have what it takes to wake up tomorrow and continue on. Maybe you're navigating loss, disappointment, and grief in this season. I want to encourage you to reach out, to connect, to find an Elizabeth or Mary among the women in your community.

Let's choose to offer courage to each other. Let's choose collaboration over comparison. Let's bear witness to the glory of God in each other. Let's be an Elizabeth or Mary to someone today. You and I were designed to flourish together.

Day 74

THEREFORE ENCOURAGE ONE ANOTHER
AND BUILD EACH OTHER UP.

I Thessalonians 5:11 NIV

TODAY, I AM FINDING GOD'S STRENGTH IN

VULNERABLE CONNECTION

A Stranger in My Own Skin

BY JEN SCHMIDT

I glanced across the room, and my eyes could sense her tension. There's nothing lonelier than walking into a room of women, scanning the whole place, and then realizing that no one has saved you a seat. There we stood—two, fifty-something-year-old women thrown back into the same realities we battled back in high school of being the new girl waiting to be welcomed in.

"Jen, I really don't want to be here right now," my friend whispered.

I'll never forget that moment.

I passionately believe in the life-giving power and gift of a simple invitation, but I've been a stranger in my own skin these days, and I'm not quite sure what to do with it. I want to understand this lonely season I'm camped in, so as my soul is parched, I reach for the only source of Living Water.

I find part of my answer in Leviticus. There's a reason God impresses the importance of showing love to strangers throughout the Old Testament. The Israelites were intimately acquainted with what it felt like to be strangers and foreigners. Once enslaved in Egypt, they experienced freedom through God's merciful rescue. And when they didn't have a home as they wandered through the wilderness, God provided food and shelter.

Clearly, God wanted the Israelites to remember their own desperate loneliness and struggles in Egypt so they could empathize and create a safe space for others to be welcomed.

This is at the core of who God is: He is the One who made a home for us, a welcome amidst our loneliness. As I'm trudging through a hard friendship season, I'm holding on to that truth. That's why I keep reaching out even when it feels like I'm on the outside looking in.

We are strangers and wanderers holding the hope of the gospel to invite and welcome. Won't you join me?

Day 75

"WHEN A STRANGER SOJOURNS WITH YOU IN YOUR LAND, YOU SHALL NOT DO HIM WRONG. YOU SHALL TREAT THE STRANGER WHO SOJOURNS WITH YOU AS THE NATIVE AMONG YOU, AND YOU SHALL LOVE HIM AS YOURSELF, FOR YOU WERE STRANGERS IN THE LAND OF EGYPT: I AM THE LORD YOUR GOD."

Leviticus 19:33–34 ESV

TODAY, I AM FINDING GOD'S STRENGTH IN

VULNERABLE CONNECTION

How to Ask and Receive

BY KARINA ALLEN

Thanksgiving found me feeling not so thankful. I didn't have plans to spend the day anywhere, and then I got sick. I spent an entire week in bed. I was miserable. Sick and alone was never what I hoped for. Yet there I was.

For the most part, I actually love being single. But one thing I loathe about single life is making every decision and taking care of myself. When I get sick, it's just me.

Lying in bed, I rehearsed all the standards lies: *I'm alone. I'm unloved. I'm unseen.* I allowed the voice of the enemy to grow louder than the voice of God.

Though I would've normally kept all my pain and struggle to myself, the Lord prompted me to share about how I was doing with my church and to ask for prayer. Multiple texts and phone calls began to come in to check on me. One friend brought me a Thanksgiving meal. Another brought me homemade chicken noodle soup. I was blown away by the love of God through their care for me.

Reaching out for help isn't easy, but it's always worth it. As I received the help from my church family that I needed, I realized how focused I had become on myself and my loneliness. I'd become fixated on lies and unmet expectations, wallowing in them. And without the Lord's nudging, I probably would've continued struggling alone, relying on my own strength instead of on God and others.

But God revealed to me that this was pride and not faith. I falsely believed I had to do it all myself, that I couldn't depend on anyone. I didn't even expect Him to provide for me.

I experienced God's grace that Thanksgiving and learned again how much I need to trust Him, abide in Him, and commune with Him and the body of Christ. I'm not alone in this, and neither are you. There is grace for us all when we humble ourselves, ask for what we need, open our hands, and receive.

Day 76

THEREFORE, WHENEVER WE HAVE THE OPPORTUNITY,
WE SHOULD DO GOOD TO EVERYONE—
ESPECIALLY TO THOSE IN THE FAMILY OF FAITH.

Galatians 6:10 NLT

TODAY, I AM FINDING GOD'S STRENGTH IN

VULNERABLE CONNECTION

Letting Yourself Be Seen

BY BECKY KEIFE

I sat on a stool in my friend Audra's kitchen, chatting about nothing, barely aware I was hiding everything. Outside on the trampoline, our kids hollered happy shouts. Audra poured me a cup of tea as Sara came in through the slider. "Everyone is playing great!"

I sipped my tea and gritted my teeth. *Get it together, Becky*, I chided myself. *You're fine.* I wanted to be fine. I *should* be fine. After all, things were fine. I had a job I loved, three healthy boys, really good friends. So why did I feel like I was spiraling into a dark pit on a sunny Friday afternoon?

Sara passed a bowl of pretzels and asked, "So how are you, friend?"

It's strange how a simple question can break through a carefully constructed dam.

"Umm. . ." was all I could get out before the tears took over.

"Oh, no! What's wrong?" my friends asked in unison.

I shrugged and futilely wiped my cheeks. My mind swirled. They waited. "I guess I'm struggling with anxiety again," I finally said. Sara rubbed my back and nodded as I continued. "It feels so stupid because I have so much to be thankful for. But I also feel really overwhelmed for the sorrow and trials other people are facing." I shared about several circumstances that were weighing on my heart: marriages crumbling, finances stretched, kids fighting cancer. It felt like there was a brick on my chest.

"You are emotional because you care," Sara offered.

"You're not stupid," Audra assured. "I think God made you sensitive so you can care for others like He does. The pain you feel is real. You don't have to minimize it or dismiss it."

Then my friends prayed for me. I don't remember the exact words, but I remember feeling cared for. Seen. Held. Like Jesus was right there with us. I would have missed out on that gift if I'd kept those tears locked away.

It's not easy being vulnerable—but it's worth it. Dare to share your honest, messy heart with a trusted friend today. Jesus will meet you there.

Day 77

HE WILL NOT BE OVERWHELMED,
BECAUSE THE LORD SUPPORTS HIM WITH HIS HAND.

Psalm 37:24 CSB

TODAY, I AM FINDING GOD'S STRENGTH IN

VULNERABLE CONNECTION

When You're Tired of Being Second Choice

BY MARY CARVER

"Mom, I feel like I'm the backup friend."

I knew exactly what she meant as soon as she said it, but I asked her to clarify anyway. And sure enough, my sweet middle schooler was afraid that she was nobody's first choice, that all her friends liked someone else better than her. She felt like they only saw her as a backup to their true preference, their first choice.

Just a couple days before that car conversation, I'd realized that I was absolutely the backup friend to someone who I'd made my first choice. "It didn't even occur to me to call you," she said without apology. It wasn't an insult, just a simple fact. And in that moment, I felt exactly twelve years old. The feeling of being overlooked or ignored by friends may have first shown up in elementary or middle school, but it never seems to go away.

As we drove down the road, I told my daughter the same two things I tell myself (over and over and over):

1. *What you're going through is hard, and I know it hurts.* I'm sorry you're feeling sad and lonely. I gave my daughter space to grieve, then sat with her in the pain to acknowledge how hard this really is.

2. *You are God's first choice.* Friends may sit with someone else in the cafeteria, forget to invite us to the movie night, or forget to add our number to the group text. We might not get picked for the team, the group project, the plus-one to the wedding, or the mastermind group. But no matter how many people deem us unworthy, God never will.

If you're feeling like a backup friend today, my heart is heavy for you. I know how that feels, and it's horrible. If you're feeling like you'll never be anyone's first choice, take heart. Don't spiral into those dark thoughts! You are someone's first choice. You're God's first choice, and you're deeply loved by Him. You are valued and treasured. You are chosen.

Day 78

EVEN BEFORE HE MADE THE WORLD,
GOD LOVED US AND CHOSE US IN CHRIST TO BE HOLY
AND WITHOUT FAULT IN HIS EYES.

Ephesians 1:4 NLT

TODAY, I AM FINDING GOD'S STRENGTH IN

VULNERABLE CONNECTION

Jesus Speaks Your Language

BY DAWN CAMP

Years ago, my dad and stepmom moved to the countryside of rural South Carolina. They live on several acres, home to an assortment of animals. No one could get close to the wary black cat who visited their property looking for food. He ate what was left for him but wanted nothing to do with those who placed it there. His trust issues probably stemmed from a life where he'd received little kindness.

Then one day, our youngest daughter sat on their back steps holding that big black cat and scratching him behind the ears. How did she charm this animal who didn't want anything to do with anybody?

She meowed at him.

That one word—one sound—crumbled the protective fortress around his feline heart. She bridged the gap when she spoke his language. From that day forward he no longer feared people but learned to trust them.

We too yearn for affection and connection, but trust doesn't come cheap. If we've been burned by past relationships, we learn to build walls or make excuses to shield ourselves from the rejection we fear.

Do you ever feel like a stranger, tolerated by the world you live in but never really fitting in? Sometimes it's hard to imagine a perfect, holy Jesus sharing our experiences, but this is not one of them. Surely no one has felt more alone, isolated, or like they didn't belong among those around them than Jesus. Resented. Mocked. Hated. Even those closest to Him didn't fully understand Him.

Because Jesus Christ experienced loneliness and grief, He can relate to ours. He is the Compassionate One who understands and sympathizes with our weaknesses. If you find yourself alone today, scared, scarred, and afraid to trust, call out His name. He speaks your language and offers the comfort your soul seeks.

Day 79

THIS HIGH PRIEST OF OURS UNDERSTANDS OUR WEAKNESSES, FOR HE FACED ALL OF THE SAME TESTINGS WE DO, YET HE DID NOT SIN. SO LET US COME BOLDLY TO THE THRONE OF OUR GRACIOUS GOD. THERE WE WILL RECEIVE HIS MERCY, AND WE WILL FIND GRACE TO HELP US WHEN WE NEED IT MOST.

Hebrews 4:15–16 NLT

TODAY, I AM FINDING GOD'S STRENGTH IN

VULNERABLE CONNECTION

The Struggle and Gift of Vulnerability

BY KARINA ALLEN

With the passing of recent birthdays, I've become more introspective. I'm in my forties and more observant about the relationships in my life. I have tons of friends that feel like family, and still . . . there is something missing.

I tend to float between friend groups. I love how God has made me a bridge and a connector of people, but sometimes it leaves me feeling a bit untethered. All the bouncing between circles can keep those friendships shallow or just beneath the surface.

What else hinders us from living truly vulnerable lives? The list seems long, but at the top is fear of rejection and fear of being misunderstood. Even though I've learned to name the fears, it's a constant battle to fight them.

But we don't have to fight these battles alone. It's our responsibility to cast down lies and renew our minds with God's Word, to carry each other's burdens, and to pray for one another, which leads to our healing.

Church has become one of the most vulnerable places in my life in recent years. It is a tender thing to watch and participate in sharing a need, asking for prayer, and allowing the Body to surround you, and believe together that God will move on someone's behalf. I have tangibly tasted and seen the goodness of our God.

That is what a life of vulnerability looks like: unhindered, free, whole, and full of love.

Vulnerability is for our good, and the Lord knows it. Our deep desire to know and be fully known by God and the Body of Christ is God-given! Showing up with vulnerability is how we walk as followers of Jesus and how we can show love and receive love. It is how we build a rich and beautiful history of trust and intimacy with God and others.

Vulnerability comes at a cost. It will cost you your pride, fear, comfort, and expectations. But the payoff can be one the sweetest gifts you'll ever experience.

Day 80

THEREFORE CONFESS YOUR SINS TO EACH OTHER AND PRAY FOR EACH OTHER SO THAT YOU MAY BE HEALED.

James 5:16 NIV

TODAY, I AM FINDING GOD'S STRENGTH IN

STEPPING INTO SOMETHING NEW

The Dusty Desert of My Heart

BY ANNA E. RENDELL

For the first time in my adult life, at forty years old, I'm attending a new church.

Last summer, due to a complicated and difficult set of circumstances, we left our church home of over twenty years. This was the church where I was married, where I baptized my babies, and where my community was. It's not an overstatement to say it was a hard, painful, sad, and downright awful season.

And then my kids asked where they would go to Sunday School.

To be honest, I wasn't ready to jump in somewhere new. The thought of joining another congregation was overwhelming and scary. When you get burned by the church, it's daunting to think of doing it again. The scars weren't even healed from the last one! But I prayed, asking the Lord if there could be new life out there for us.

We made a couple of calls, watched a few services online, visited in person, and enrolled in Sunday School at a church right in our community. Our family was welcomed warmly, and it's been a soft place to land. A stream in the dry, dusty desert of my heart.

It didn't feel like God would do something new in this church-shaped hole. Silly, I know, but true. It was painful to think that I'd spent decades serving, pouring out, leading, and worshipping, just to have it all end. But when the proverbial walls of my church crumbled, God remained.

It was never about losing Him. It was always about following close enough to hear His call for the next step, for the new thing He promised.

Maybe it's not your church. Maybe it's a cherished relationship, now strained. Maybe it's a beloved career, suddenly on the rocks. Maybe it's an old habit that just won't die.

Whatever it is, God is in the business of creating beauty right from ashes. Painful as it may be, it could be time to walk away and let it burn, friend. God's got a new thing already in the works.

Day 81

TO ALL WHO MOURN IN ISRAEL,
HE WILL GIVE A CROWN OF BEAUTY FOR ASHES,
A JOYOUS BLESSING INSTEAD OF MOURNING,
FESTIVE PRAISE INSTEAD OF DESPAIR.

Isaiah 61:3 NLT

TODAY, I AM FINDING GOD'S STRENGTH IN

When You Find Yourself Asking, "Now What?"

BY JENNIFER DUKES LEE

We've gone through much change lately. At every turn, it seemed like we were stepping into something new. First, Dad passed away. It seemed impossible that this world had been emptied of his daily presence. I found myself wanting to pick up the phone to tell him the latest news, or to hear his voice, but that couldn't happen.

Then, our older daughter moved overseas to study. While we celebrated her sense of collegiate adventure, the alarming nature of time's swift march struck us with unexpected force. *Hadn't we just enrolled her in kindergarten?* And finally, our younger daughter left for college, leaving my husband and me inside our empty, echoing nest.

I worried that all that change—all at once—would create a vacuum, sucking up so much laughter, so many conversations, and the center points on which our worlds pivoted.

When it all quieted down, my husband and I turned to each and asked, "Well, now what?" Now what would we do with our time, our evenings, our social lives, our priorities? Now what would we do in this strange Land of Something New?

In response to all of those "now whats," we started . . . "now-whatting."

"Now-whatting" took us on new adventures. We cooked new foods in our new air fryer. We've eaten out a lot, probably more than we should. (Note the theme of food.)

We told stories of Dad and FaceTimed our daughters. We found ourselves saying to one another, "I really like spending time with you!"

A sudden switch or rerouting can upend you. You may find yourself lifting your face to God, asking, "Now what?" Stepping into something new can be scary, for sure. Yet the world opens up, beckoning you to embrace the adventure with a new hobby, a class, a new perspective, or wherever your "now-whatting" leads you.

May you embrace your own kind of "now-whatting," where you sense God drawing you from the emptiness into a new and lovely season of life.

Day 82

"SEE, I AM DOING A NEW THING! NOW IT SPRINGS UP; DO YOU NOT PERCEIVE IT? I AM MAKING A WAY IN THE WILDERNESS AND STREAMS IN THE WASTELAND."

Isaiah 43:19 NIV

TODAY, I AM FINDING GOD'S STRENGTH IN

When You're Facing a Lonelier Holiday

BY KRISTEN STRONG

I awake on Easter morning with a sad sigh rather than the joy I desperately want to feel. My husband and three college kids are either traveling or can't get away from school. So, for the first time in more than twenty-five years, I'm attending Easter service by myself.

Having no family around on a major holiday isn't a new concept for a former military spouse like me. Still, familiarity with it doesn't mean I like it, especially in the same year I became an official empty nester.

I arrive at church and find my friend, Maria, who'd invited me to sit with her family during the service. We belt out, "Christ the Lord Is Risen Today!" and listen to the Easter message. Afterward, we gab a good deal, and my heart lightens a little.

After church, another friend, Aimée, invites me to have Easter dinner with her family. I fill myself on ham, beans, and biscuits, oh yes. Sitting at Aimée's table, I also fill myself on the comradery of a family who isn't my own yet blesses me as if they are.

It turns out family can also be found in friends.

Author Ann Voskamp writes, "If the tomb wasn't empty, our hearts would be."[2] It's true my home was much emptier this past Easter, but at the end of the day, my heart wasn't. Would I have loved to have had my husband and kids around? Absolutely. But the emptier space brought by their absence also brought me closer to the knowledge that Jesus emptied Himself on the cross so I could be filled. And fill me this Easter He did, through time and conversation with friends. What's more, my quieter Easter gave space for me to know afresh that Jesus died and rose again so I could be included and known.

The tomb is empty, so I am not. Whether we spend the holidays in a crowd or at a table for one, we are seen. This is heart-filling truth indeed.

And this truth comforts us because while a holiday may be different, it can still be good.

---

2 Ann Voskamp (@AnnVoskamp), Instagram caption, April 9, 2023, https://www.instagram.com/p/Cq0Ipg3OI0E/.

Day 83

GOD SETS THE LONELY IN FAMILIES.

Psalm 68:6 NIV

TODAY, I AM FINDING GOD'S STRENGTH IN

STEPPING INTO SOMETHING NEW

His Mercies Are New Every Minute

BY RACHEL MARIE KANG

I'm in my car and turning onto the interstate that takes me over the lake. I like the way the water sparkles—like a mirror, always reflecting the light of the good sun.

As the water sparkles, I think about something that younger me never realized. Right here in my car, with nothing mystical or magnificent happening, I feel God and His presence. I think of the passage of Scripture that carried me through my weary, teenage years: the steadfast love of God never stops, and His mercies are new every morning.

Long gone are my adolescent years when I'd cry myself to sleep, unsure of God's mercy and overwhelmed with the weight of life. Desperate to believe that God's mercy was really for me, I'd cry my heart out just before sleep so many nights, only to wake up puffy-eyed and hoping the newness that I felt from waking to a new day was God's way of waking me to new mercies.

Looking back, I now see that God's mercy didn't just come to me every morning; it also carried me through every night and every minute of every day. And if I held on to Him then, I can hold on to Him this minute, never needing to hold out for the morning to wash me anew. I can recall His mercies to my mind now, right here in this car driving over the lake that sparkles with the light of the good sun.

Wherever you are today, God's mercies are available to you. Whether you're raging over the injustices in your life or in the world, or you're weary from the everyday mundane. Whether you cry yourself to sleep at night or bemoan when morning comes, you can count on God's new mercies to meet you.

His mercies are new every minute, every millisecond, stretching wide and reaching deep to cover us for any reason . . . at any time, in any place. You can step into each new day knowing God's love meets you and carries you.

Day 84

THE STEADFAST LOVE OF THE LORD NEVER CEASES;
HIS MERCIES NEVER COME TO AN END;
THEY ARE NEW EVERY MORNING.

Lamentations 3:22–23 ESV

TODAY, I AM FINDING GOD'S STRENGTH IN

Perfection Is Not an Option

BY MELISSA ZALDIVAR

I had no idea what I was doing, but I didn't want anyone *else* to know that. Graduate school was wrapping up, my friends were making plans for moving to far corners of the world, and I still didn't know what was next. I'm a list-maker by nature, so I pulled out a whiteboard and grabbed a marker, writing down every dream job I could possibly think of. Clearly, organization was key, and quick success was on its way.

But then, momentum started to dwindle. I sent out strategic emails but was met with crickets, and that's when I realized: we can scheme and plan, but really? God is the one who directs our steps. Planning and intentionality are good things, but when we put our trust in them, we're likely going to be let down by our own efforts.

Part of the way through my make-a-plan process, I pulled out a marker and wrote in big letters at the top: PERFECTION IS NOT AN OPTION. While it felt strange to say it, those words gave me the freedom to trust Jesus and know that just because things feel a bit complicated doesn't mean I'm doomed.

As days turned to weeks and months, I kept coming back to that phrase, leaning on the reality that Jesus promises that we will have trouble and conflict, but He will be present in the midst of it. It's His nearness in the middle of the struggle that carries us through. Jesus Himself is our reward!

When it comes to diving into something new, it's almost never straightforward. We can put so much pressure on ourselves to deliver a certain outcome that we miss the fact that God is inviting us to trust Him and to trust the process of this season.

My job hunt brought ups and downs and all arounds, and in the end, it was longer and harder than I would have chosen. But I was certain that God was in the center of things, which brought peace when it was time to take the next step.

Day 85

YOU WILL KEEP IN PERFECT PEACE THOSE WHOSE MINDS ARE STEADFAST, BECAUSE THEY TRUST IN YOU.

Isaiah 26:3 NIV

TODAY, I AM FINDING GOD'S STRENGTH IN

Don't Let Old Jeans Make You Keep Looking Back

BY SIMI JOHN

I recently found my favorite pair of jeans from college. When I tried to put them on, I quickly realized they weren't coming up past my thighs. I stared at the long mirror on the back of my closet door, examining the curves of my hips, the cellulite on my thighs, and the stretchmarks on my waist. This body wasn't how I remembered it. Tears, anger, and frustration flowed as I peered at my reflection.

Later that week, I was working with an older gentleman who needed physical therapy for weakness and balance. He reminisced about how he'd played college sports and lamented how now his body was practically useless. I urged him to focus on his present abilities and how far he'd come in therapy. I encouraged him to honor his body for what it was today instead of comparing it to its past.

When I saw my old jeans later, I realized so much had changed in twelve years, including my pant size: marriage, a career, two babies, travel—I'd lived so much life! I decided to take my own advice and honor who I am today. I wouldn't resent my body for not meeting an unrealistic goal or punish it through dieting. I would ditch the old jeans and stop looking back. Then I thought of Lot's wife.

She was promised to be saved from destruction if she fled without looking back. Sadly, she looked back and turned into a pillar of salt. She had a guaranteed future, but she glanced back at what had brought her comfort instead of focusing on what was ahead.

Often the "glory days" or the "good ol' days" make it hard to find contentment in the present. It's hard to step into an unknown future when we live in the comfort of yesterday's memories.

Friend, God's not done with you. He isn't disappointed that you're different today than you were ten years ago. He wants you just the way you are, right now—cellulite and all. So no more turning back.

Day 86

FORGETTING WHAT LIES BEHIND AND REACHING FORWARD TO WHAT LIES AHEAD, I PRESS ON TOWARD THE GOAL FOR THE PRIZE OF THE UPWARD CALL OF GOD IN CHRIST JESUS.

Philippians 3:13–14 NASB1995

TODAY, I AM FINDING GOD'S STRENGTH IN

Provision on the Way to the Promised Land

BY ALIZA LATTA

I was three months into my new job in full-time ministry. I had gone from making a decent income working in journalism to fundraising my salary as a local missionary. When I accepted the position, I wasn't afraid. I welcomed the challenge. I was right where God wanted me.

Except . . . fundraising was much harder than I'd anticipated. Bills kept arriving. Rent kept needing to be paid. Groceries were more expensive every time I went to the store.

Anxiety gripped my heart like a squeezing boa constrictor. What if I'd made a huge mistake? What if I couldn't fundraise? What if I was left with no job and no money?

I stood in my kitchen and cried out to God. "Why did I leave my old job? Why did I think I could do this? I want to go back! I don't want this new season anymore."

Immediately, I felt God kindly and tenderly reprimand me.

You sound like the Israelites, I sensed God tell me. *You want to go back to Egypt. Back to the place where you think you'll have garlic and leeks and meat. But I'm taking you to the Promised Land. I'll provide for you every step of the way.*

I felt sheepish. He was right. God's always right. I had complained for the longest time, asking Him to get me out of my prior job, begging Him to bring me into something new. And He did. But as soon as the new season got hard, I was begging Him to take me back to where I'd come from!

I thought because my new season felt like it was directly from God, it would somehow be easier. But just because something is from God, doesn't mean it's always comfortable or without struggle. It does mean God will be with us every step of the way.

New jobs, new relationships, new life seasons—new anything—can be scary and uncomfortable. But it's there that you'll find God's presence and guidance. He's the God of new mercies. You can trust Him.

Day 87

AND MY GOD WILL MEET ALL YOUR NEEDS ACCORDING TO THE RICHES OF HIS GLORY IN CHRIST JESUS.

Philippians 4:19 NIV

TODAY, I AM FINDING GOD'S STRENGTH IN

Blinking Cursors and Desert Seasons

BY ANNA E. RENDELL

My tea is hot, soft piano music plays, crickets chirp outside, and the trees rustle in the breeze. The setting perfect, I open my laptop. The cursor blinks, expecting a next move. But I have no next move. I'm totally empty, utterly spent, not a word to be found in my brain or heart or fingers.

There's been no great catastrophe, nothing life altering to make my heart shrivel. I'm simply weary with the daily: the diapers and too-fast days and spilled juice, meetings and deadlines, and full squares on the calendar.

There's no room to just be, and I'm drying up.

A desert season of the heart is scary. How am I supposed to teach my children, write, lead a devotion in my MOPS group, and help a friend if I am running on fumes? A refueling of my heart seems impossible because there's no time to go sit in a quiet sanctuary, swing my feet off a lake dock, or bask in a field of wildflowers. A perfect setting is fleeting anyway, and this is real life. Real life is messy and full of blinking cursors. Real life is loud, and sometimes I'm afraid that if I stop and be still, underneath it all there won't be anything worth saying.

I forget that God calls us to stillness, to deep calmness. That He speaks most clearly when I'm most quiet. That even in my desert, He sparkles.

When we're most dried up, God can do some of His finest work.

Real life beckons us to be still and know. Our hearts may be covered in a thick coating of desert dust. We may be scared. We may not see that new springs of joy can flow. We may see nothing but wasteland, from horizon to horizon of our lives.

But even then, God is at work creating—in us and for us. He's working. And despite the blinking cursor and volume of our real-life noise, we can be still and know that truth.

Day 88

THE LAME WILL LEAP LIKE A DEER,
AND THOSE WHO CANNOT SPEAK WILL SING FOR JOY!
SPRINGS WILL GUSH FORTH IN THE WILDERNESS,
AND STREAMS WILL WATER THE WASTELAND.

Isaiah 35:6 NLT

TODAY, I AM FINDING GOD'S STRENGTH IN

In Limbo, but Not Alone

BY LUCRETIA BERRY

I can't go back to church," my friend confessed as we stood in my driveway. Before heading back to her car, we'd paused for an impromptu check-in. She was obviously wrestling with something. As I listened to her nervously explain, anticipating a negative reaction from me, I could tell she felt alone in her experience.

I asked her if she felt in limbo, in between places. She was relieved to hear words that resonated with her soul and experience.

A few years ago, I stood in someone else's driveway listening as a couple shared with me that they couldn't go back to their church. As they professed their convictions, I grieved their experience. You see, God let me know that this was going to happen. In what felt like a whisper from God's Spirit, He gave me a "heads up" that more people would feel compelled to move on from their local churches, but He also let me know that I shouldn't worry because His goodness would always prevail.

So when my friend awkwardly poured out her convictions and anxiety onto my driveway, I wasn't shocked. This kind of impromptu confession had become a familiar experience. I had not only listened in driveways but also on sidewalks after events, at the end of business meetings, and in the corner during a social gathering.

The good news is that in the absence of certainty, God is fully present and magnified.

God is in this in-between place; He's in our questions, our searching, our courageous moving and shifting. God is with us in the driveway as we grasp for assurance, direction, and protection.

Whether we meet in a church building on Sundays or a coffee shop on Wednesdays, we need time together to be vulnerable and to be validated. We also need to be in each other's presence to stir life within one another. We need close proximity to snuff out isolation. Gathering brings definition to the in-between place and reminds us not to be afraid. Meeting together helps reconcile the limbo and calls it good!

Feeling uncertain about the way forward is okay. But being in limbo doesn't mean you have to be alone.

Day 89

GIVE YOUR BURDENS TO THE LORD,
AND HE WILL TAKE CARE OF YOU.
HE WILL NOT PERMIT THE GODLY TO SLIP AND FALL.

Psalm 55:22 NLT

TODAY, I AM FINDING GOD'S STRENGTH IN

Figuring Out Fresh Starts

BY MARY CARVER

As we ate our takeout, my husband talked *again* about our daughter's behavior. I confessed something I'd realized about the situation. "I can't start fresh," I whispered. "My frustrations just keep building, and there's no break, no relief, no blank slate."

We recognized that our short fuses were contributing to the problem, but we didn't know how to fix it. And I knew that this fresh start thing was part of it. Without a fresh start, there's no forgiveness. I couldn't find my way out of the garbage heap of anger. I couldn't see the light of grace. Though I admitted the problem, I kept feeling angry and frustrated. I kept losing my temper with my disobedient and disrespectful little girl. I didn't know how to stop feeling that way.

One day as I lamented our struggle to her first-grade teacher, she suggested we use the color-coded behavior chart at home that they use in the classroom. I knew the color chart was important to my daughter because every afternoon she would tell me what color she was on: a green day was good, average, nothing to see here. A yellow (or even red) day meant she was crying before she even got into the car. A blue or pink day, though, was cause for celebration!

We implemented the color chart at home, and it worked. *It worked!* But not for the reason I expected. What made the difference was that at the end of the day, no matter how ugly or difficult or *red* it was, I moved my daughter's pin back to green. Every day started fresh. It had the potential to be better or worse, but it started on green.

Something about physically moving that clothespin back to green on our chart reset *my* heart too. Even after the worst days, that simple gesture lifted a burden from my heart. It helped me love her better . . . again. And it reminded me that because of God's great mercy, I get to start on green each day too.

Day 90

"I HAVE SWEPT AWAY YOUR TRANSGRESSIONS LIKE A CLOUD, AND YOUR SINS LIKE A MIST. RETURN TO ME, FOR I HAVE REDEEMED YOU."

Isaiah 44:22 CSB

TODAY, I AM FINDING GOD'S STRENGTH IN

Nothing Is Too Small

BY KAYLA CRAIG

Fireworks boomed and bellowed. We weren't expecting them to be so close—or so loud. My husband and I escaped from the front lawn of the fireworks show, herding our overwhelmed kids and shaking dog to the parking lot. When we arrived to the safety of our van, I let myself exhale.

We buckled the youngest kids into their car seats, and in that split second, our tiny fluffball escaped. Flooded with fear, she ran as fast as she could into the black night. My husband chased after her, waving down friends to help. My job was to stay with the kids. I expected our crew to come back soon with the dog in their arms.

They didn't. We waited. And waited.

I told the kids it would be okay, but I wasn't so sure. I started to hear whimpers from the back seat. Tears began to pool in my eyes too. I felt helpless. It was a high-traffic area. My thoughts hurdled to worst-case scenarios. I decided to drive around the neighborhood, rolling down my window and asking if anyone had seen a little white dog. No one had.

My kids sobbed. The fireworks display ended, and we found ourselves in a rush of traffic. My hope diminished. I felt a little embarrassed praying about our lost dog, but it was my honest prayer. I was heartsick for my kids, for feeling like I failed them and our family. Exhausted, I wiped tears from my cheek and prayed . . . hard.

I tried to take a back way to escape the traffic, and in a last-ditch effort, I rolled down my window near a man who was walking on the sidewalk. "Excuse me, have you seen a small dog?"

Hands on his knees, he looked up at me and nodded. I realized he was out of breath. "I just chased her down," he shouted back. "She's at my house. She's safe."

I can't pretend to understand the mystery of prayer, but in that moment, I know I experienced God's grace. Nothing is too small, no night is too dark, to invite God into.

Day 91

CAST ALL YOUR ANXIETY ON HIM
BECAUSE HE CARES FOR YOU.

I Peter 5:7 NIV

TODAY, I AM FINDING GOD'S STRENGTH IN

Pour out Your Heart on the Page

BY TASHA JUN

Most days after school, I spent fifteen minutes writing notes to God. I think I was twelve or thirteen. I didn't even call myself a Christian then. But every afternoon, I peeled open a small, light-blue journal and begged God for friends.

There was a group of girls who gave themselves a special name, and being part of their group was the hope of every junior-high girl I knew. So I'd sit down and scribble my heart out to God: *God, please let me be invited into this group. When I see so-and-so after fifth period, please let her ask me to join.*

Day after day after day.

Finally, at some point, I gave up. I gave up on hoping to be invited in and on whether or not God cared. What I didn't realize is that before I gave up, I'd been building a little habit.

Years later, it was almost instinctual for me to open up a journal and write my heart out. The God I wondered about years before—the One I thought didn't care and didn't answer me, the One I was pouring my heart out to—was the One I now knew. And I already knew how to talk to Him! Throughout those years of honesty and unanswered prayers, I was building a posture I had no idea I would come back to like a muscle with memory.

Think about your most honest journal entry. What if you addressed it to God?

God wants our honest feelings. Our emotions and true thoughts aren't too much. They aren't a liability; they are a pathway to intimacy and true growth.

The anxiety and worries that wake us in the night have a welcome place to go. The contents of our hearts do not have to stay inside and hidden. What would you say to God if you were twelve or thirteen again? What would you say if you knew God's ears and heart were wide, wide open?

Day 92

RISE DURING THE NIGHT AND CRY OUT.
POUR OUT YOUR HEARTS LIKE WATER TO THE LORD.

Lamentations 2:19 NLT

TODAY, I AM FINDING GOD'S STRENGTH IN

More Than I Longed For

BY LUCRETIA BERRY

Father, I stretch my hands to Thee. No other help I know. If you withdraw Thy strength from me, ah . . . where shall I go?" Every child, including me, could imitate this prayer with the same eloquence expressed by our church elder who passionately recited it every Sunday during the eleven o'clock worship service. But I wondered, *Will I know how to pray like that on my own when I grow up?* I presumed such poetic prose adorned with *thee's*, *thou's*, and *thy's* were God's preferred expression of prayer.

I longed to pray like that. Praying with such style and propriety would surely suggest that I was connected to God—that I was special to Him, right?

Over the years, as I searched to have a place in God's heart, I found that I was already there—established and created by Him! All along, God had been patiently waiting for me to fully understand that I was His. Once I was fully conscious of my connection—because His Spirit lived in me—I knew that whatever prayers poured from me were a reflection of His heart.

I realized there was no need for prestigious prose in prayer and that God passionately regards those who are disregarded in our world. As I prayed God's heart, His words were like water quenching thirsty deserts, a mighty current powerfully and gently smoothing rough places in my heart.

My prayers are occasionally poetic, but they're more often gritty, raw, and naked—whispered and shouted in private, too unpolished for public consumption. One moment, they're tears of lament, and the next tears of joy! This is honest prayer. It can also be silent, listening, and aligning. And when there are no words to communicate God's heart, I groan or roar or laugh or simply wave my hand.

God doesn't expect us to perform poetic prose when we pray. As I pray honestly, reflecting God's heart, I'm certain that I belong to Him. So do you.

Day 93

LIKEWISE THE SPIRIT HELPS US IN OUR WEAKNESS. FOR WE DO NOT KNOW WHAT TO PRAY FOR AS WE OUGHT, BUT THE SPIRIT HIMSELF INTERCEDES FOR US WITH GROANINGS TOO DEEP FOR WORDS.

Romans 8:26 ESV

TODAY, I AM FINDING GOD'S STRENGTH IN

Bringing Every Feeling to Jesus

BY ALIZA LATTA

The ache came out of nowhere. I was sitting on the beach with people I love and a novel I'd been waiting to read. But then a pang shot through me—a pang of loneliness, an ache of longing. It made no sense for me to be lonely while surrounded by people in a place I love. And yet, the ache was there.

I've begun to wonder if maybe I'm not the only one with the ache. Maybe all of us have this ache deep within. Maybe the ache isn't dependent on loneliness but on the simple fact that being a human is exhausting and is often accompanied by a union of joy and sorrow.

Jesus knows exactly what it's like to be an exhausted human. He got tired and sad, just like we do. And Jesus knows everything about our individual lives. He knows our disappointments, shame, embarrassment, discouragement, and doubts. For us, these feelings can be complicated. We think we need to figure things out before bringing our hearts to Jesus. But Jesus already knows it all. Why would we keep these confusing parts of our lives from Him?

I decided to come to Jesus in prayer. I brought Him my achy heart and was met with the deepest compassion.

I talked to Jesus throughout that whole day at the beach. It wasn't fancy. I simply prayed: *Jesus, the ache is back. Jesus, the ache has returned.*

A huge part of me wanted Jesus to fix it, to sweep it away with a touch of His hands. But He didn't fix it. Instead, He walked beside me. As I got into my car and drove home, the ache accompanied me. But so did Jesus.

No matter what we're feeling—no matter how embarrassing or shameful or discouraging—we can bring it all to Jesus. We don't have to be afraid of our emotions. We can gather them up, handing our fistful of feelings over to the Lord who already sees us . . . and be met with compassion and deep love.

Day 94

DO NOT BE ANXIOUS ABOUT ANYTHING,
BUT IN EVERY SITUATION, BY PRAYER AND PETITION,
WITH THANKSGIVING, PRESENT YOUR REQUESTS TO GOD.

Philippians 4:6 NIV

TODAY, I AM FINDING GOD'S STRENGTH IN

The Best Little Four-Word Prayer

BY BARB ROOSE

In Psalm 69, King David shares a precious, simple, four-word prayer that you and I might need: "Save me, O God."

This little powerhouse prayer was written at an unknown time in King David's life. David had a lot of drama where this prayer could have applied, whether when he was running for his life or dealing with his own wrongdoings, his sons' rebellion, or his daughter's sexual assault. David's prayer continues as he uses the analogy that the "floodwaters are up to [his] neck." Does that resonate with you? David isn't sugarcoating his situation, nor is he beating around the bush about what he needs.

Just four powerful words: Save me, O God.

Even if you don't need them right now, tuck these four little words away for the future. Depending on how you grew up, those four little words may not feel like enough. You might be wondering if God will overlook a prayer that small or short.

God isn't looking for eloquence or length when it comes to our prayers. Longer prayers don't make you more spiritual. Likewise, fancy words don't guarantee that you're praying in faith. Prayer is prayer. So, David's, *"Save Me, O God"* demonstrates two principles of what I call "good and gritty prayers": short and honest.

God sees you right now. Not only that, but He is also present with you in a posture of love, never condemnation. Even more, God promises that His help is on the way. However, He rescues in *His* all-powerful way, not ours. If you do call out, "Save me, O God," remember that God works differently than we do. Let's put our confidence in trusting that God will save us, rather than get picky or panicky about how or when He will do it. If you need God's help today, open your heart and mind wide and be willing to accept God's help no matter the outcome.

God is with you in whatever you're going through. Whether your rescue looks like repair, restoration, redemption, or eternal resurrection, God will be there every step of the way.

Day 95

SAVE ME, O GOD, FOR THE FLOODWATERS ARE UP TO MY NECK.

Psalm 69:1 NLT

TODAY, I AM FINDING GOD'S STRENGTH IN

Cleaning Up Broken Glass

BY TASHA JUN

Last week, my oldest dropped a drinking glass. I watched his eyes pop like a puffer fish as the blue Ball jar transformed into a million shards and flew across every inch of our slate tile kitchen floor.

After immediately quarantining myself in the kitchen, I shooed my kids out. Then I stood there, looking at all the fragments and splinters. I wasn't sad over losing the drinking glass; I was amazed by what it had become.

Sometimes life feels like standing in a room surrounded by sharp splinters and rough-edged remnants of what was.

Overwhelmed, I stood still in the middle of the mess and just stared. Then I whispered the word "help." Even a paltry prayer for help can awaken my hope that God is ever-present and unsurprised by the wreckage in my every day.

Pick up one jagged piece and then another, He whispered back to me in the kitchen that day. So I bent low to see the tiny pieces up close and started cleaning up, slow and steady.

Despite my orders to stay away, one of my sons offered help by bringing a bag for the glass and asking if he could get the vacuum. Another son brought bandages when he heard me yelp in pain after stepping on glass. And our littlest came closer with a box of tissues in hand just like others have done for her when she's hurt or sad.

Moments like these give us space to see our needs and care for each other. They train us to give and receive love. Grace always weaves its way in and through the wreckage and the wounds.

Sometimes all we can do is stare at the mess, ask for help, and wait to see new mercies winnow through, making us wonder again. When we bend down low, go slow, and look for one piece to pick up, we'll find that one tiny piece after another become one small space after another made safe again.

Day 96

IN MY DESPERATION I PRAYED, AND THE LORD LISTENED;
HE SAVED ME FROM ALL MY TROUBLES.

Psalm 34:6 NLT

TODAY, I AM FINDING GOD'S STRENGTH IN

How to Pray When Healing Doesn't Come

BY DORINA LAZO GILMORE-YOUNG

When my husband received a stage-four cancer diagnosis, our friends and family gathered at our house to pray. On one of the scariest days of my life, I was strengthened by their fervent prayers. But after my husband's death, I wrestled with God. Hundreds of people had prayed for his healing, and it hadn't come.

Why continue to pray when our prayers weren't answered?

I struggled to know how to pray, how to proceed. My faith was strong, but my heart felt fragile. My prayers escaped as desperate whispers on the darkest nights of grief.

Over time, I was reminded that just because we pray doesn't mean we get our way. We don't punch in on a prayer clock to gain a certain outcome. In fact, the purpose of prayer isn't to persuade God to do things our way; it's to draw close to our Father and sit in His presence.

Jesus models this for us when He prayed at the Mount of Olives before His betrayal. In His honest prayer, Jesus shows us how to express our hearts to God and how to pray with trust for His will to be done. In Luke 22:41–42, Jesus asked God if there was someway—anyway—that He could avoid the cross, but in the end, Jesus put His fate in God's hands when He ended the prayer with "not my will, but yours, be done" (ESV).

My heart shifted over time as I realized the purpose of prayer is to connect more intimately with the Father and trust His plan and guidance. In my grief, He was close to me. He wept with me. He offered comfort when the ache was heavy and the future seemed hopeless. Now I embrace the sweetness of knowing I can surrender the outcome of every single prayer to a capable and all-knowing God.

Years now after my husband's death, I'm grateful. Not for his death or our suffering but for the ways God has transformed our grief for His glory. I'm grateful God guided me step by step, day by day, prayer by prayer, back into His arms.

Day 97

AND HE WITHDREW FROM THEM ABOUT A STONE'S THROW, AND KNELT DOWN AND PRAYED, SAYING, "FATHER, IF YOU ARE WILLING, REMOVE THIS CUP FROM ME. NEVERTHELESS, NOT MY WILL, BUT YOURS, BE DONE."

Luke 22:41–42 ESV

TODAY, I AM FINDING GOD'S STRENGTH IN

HONEST PRAYER

When You Don't Have the Words to Pray

BY KAYLA CRAIG

When a respiratory virus attacked my three-year-old daughter's lungs, she relied on a ventilator to keep her alive. I sat by her too-big hospital bed, searching for reminders of life as her sedated body struggled under the weight of drips and machines.

I couldn't hold my baby. I could only sit and wait. I wanted to pray but had not one ounce of energy to muster anything. And honestly, I wanted to yell at God.

I thought, too, of the suffering that people experience every day. I lamented. I doubted. I wrestled with fears, and I wasn't sure if I could hand them over to God. I didn't know how. So, I held on to them instead. I couldn't hold my daughter. But I could embrace my anger and fear.

On one of my days at home, I checked the mailbox. Bills and junk mail spilled out, but there was a package nestled inside too. A book of prayers.

I didn't have to have it all together. I didn't have to have the perfect quiet space to center my thoughts—the beeps and buzzes of medical machines would do. All I had to do was open the book and read, recite, and repeat until I felt my heart rate begin to calm, until I was no longer tensing my shoulders, until I could release the breaths I'd been holding for too long.

We don't need the perfect location or perfect circumstances or perfect words to pray.

When everything crumbled, the prayers of another voice comforted me. And as I prayed, the written words—authored by a sister in Christ who I will probably never meet—became my own pleas and petitions, jumped off the page and nestled into my soul. As I learned in those thin spaces in the intensive care unit, the body of Christ says: *You don't have the words? Here, take mine.*

What a gift that we don't have to have just the right words for God to listen. God is already listening. God is all around us, and holy moments live in the ordinary and extraordinary times in our lives.

Day 98

LET US THEN APPROACH GOD'S THRONE OF GRACE WITH CONFIDENCE, SO THAT WE MAY RECEIVE MERCY AND FIND GRACE TO HELP US IN OUR TIME OF NEED.

Hebrews 4:16 NIV

TODAY, I AM FINDING GOD'S STRENGTH IN

HONEST PRAYER

Crying Out to God

BY TASHA JUN

Some days I still feel like the fifth-grade me who ran to my room and buried my face in a pillow. Sobs spilled from my eyes like water released from a dam. Salty tears fastened clumps of thick, black hair to my cheeks.

It was in those moments that I called out to the God I did not yet know. I pleaded for Him to come and change the painful circumstances I faced and challenged Him to show up if He was really there and cared. We had just moved back to the States after living overseas. I was grieving what our family lost in the move, and angry that I couldn't go back to what was.

Decades later, I now know God and pray mostly calm, level-headed prayers, but it's the raw moments—when I've come to the end of myself—that stand out. Like my ten-year-old self, I still come face-to-face with pain, challenge, and brokenness in and around me: the sadness that sometimes results in angry outbursts, the heartache I see in those I love, the irreconcilable relationships everywhere I look. In these desperate moments, I again lay myself down in a salty-faced surrender, asking Jesus to come.

Back in fifth grade, my circumstances didn't change in the immediate way I wanted them to. But now I can look back and see an irreplaceable beauty standing right next to what only felt like ugly, unfiltered prayers at the time. I see hope being written into the lines of those memories that I wished away.

God could have done exactly what I asked of Him, but if He did, perhaps I would've begun to take Him for a genie in a bottle. I wanted a miracle, but what I really needed was a Divine Presence, my Ever-Present God. I despised my weakness and inability to change things, but I needed to learn just how reliable His strength is.

What's causing you to cry out to God today? Cry into your pillow if needed. Pour out your heart to God. And keep looking for the gift of His unfailing strength and care, right where you are.

EVENING, MORNING AND NOON I CRY OUT IN DISTRESS, AND HE HEARS MY VOICE.

Psalm 55:17 NIV

TODAY, I AM FINDING GOD'S STRENGTH IN

Prayer in the Era of Self-Help

BY JENNIFER DUKES LEE

When things go wrong, my first instinct isn't always a posture of prayer. Instead, I often adopt a posture of self-help. I act as if my theology is something along the lines of, "I've got this," instead of, "God's got this."

You might not say it out loud, but deep within you, you might be thinking, "God is great and all, but if I want something done, I'll have to do it myself." And let's face it, so many of us have poured out our hearts to God, only to feel like our prayers were just an echo in the darkness.

I found myself falling into this way of thinking recently when one of my children was facing a particularly difficult challenge that had us all in tears. I sat awake many nights in a row devising plans to "fix the problem." I thought about ways to confront, correct, or control what was happening.

One morning, after a particularly long night, I was studying a verse in John. "In this world you will have trouble. But take heart! I have overcome the world" (John 16:33 NIV).

I kept looking at the tiny, three-word exclamation in the middle of that verse: "But take heart!" Jesus didn't say, "Take matters into your own hands." He didn't say, "Take control." He said, "Take heart."

Taking heart is not a posture of self-help. It's the posture of humility. Indeed, it's the posture of prayer. Prayer is the acknowledgement that we're not running the show—God is. It's a way of saying, "I trust Your ways more than mine, Lord."

One prayer really can change everything, so don't underestimate the power of your prayers. Don't fall for the lie that your prayers have to be said a certain way to count. Don't give up asking. Not now! God hears you, and no prayer is ever, ever wasted. Ask and ask again because even when our prayers don't change our circumstances, those prayers are changing us.

Don't give up now. You are never as powerful as that moment when you fall to your knees in prayer.

Day 100

"IN THIS WORLD YOU WILL HAVE TROUBLE. BUT TAKE HEART! I HAVE OVERCOME THE WORLD."

John 16:33 NIV

TODAY, I AM FINDING GOD'S STRENGTH IN

Contributors

Becky Keife is the Community and Editorial Manager for (in)courage, a passionate speaker, and the author of Bible studies and books, including *The Simple Difference*. She and her husband live near Los Angeles where they enjoy hiking on shady trails with their three spirited sons.

Karina Allen is devoted to helping women live out their unique calling and build authentic community through the practical application of Scripture in an approachable, winsome manner.

Lucretia Berry is the founder of Brownicity, whose mission is to foster education designed to inspire a culture of justice and belonging for all. Her books, including, *Hues of You*, promote racial healing and understanding. Lucretia and husband, Nathan, are raising three daughters in North Carolina.

Kaitlyn Bouchillon is a Virtual Assistant, book launch manager, and storyteller who writes about discovering God's goodness in the ordinary and faithfulness in the difficult. She loves good books, deep conversations, and iced vanilla lattes. Kaitlyn is the author of *Even If Not*.

Dawn Camp shares God's gift of essential oils in her newest releases, *My Essential Oil Companion* and *It All Began in a Garden*. She is a photographer, Mom to eight, and Mimi to seven. Dawn enjoys movie nights with her husband and steaming cups of Earl Grey.

Mary Carver writes and speaks with humor and honesty, encouraging women with truth found in unexpected places. She hosts a podcast about pop culture and faith and is the author of multiple (in)courage books including *Women of Courage* and *Journey to the Cross*.

Grace P. Cho is a Korean American writer, poet, speaker, and editor. She is a coauthor of *Empowered: More of Him for All of You* and the author of the (in)courage Bible studies *Courageous Influence* and *Create in Me a Heart of Wisdom*.

Kayla Craig is the author of *Every Season Sacred* and *To Light Their Way*. A former journalist, she's adamant abou paying attention and staying curious. Kayla explores what it looks like to see God in all things in her work as a writer and podcaster.

Michele Cushatt is a storyteller at heart, a three-time, head-and-neck cancer survivor, and mama to children "from hard places." In her newest book, *A Faith That Will Not Fail*, Michele helps people build a faith strong enough to endure any season.

Robin Dance is an author, aging specialist, and life plan advisor whose relatable encouragement inspires others in person, in print, and online. Southern as sugar-shocked tea, she's an empty-nesting mom, married to her college sweetheart, and living in the heart of Georgia.

Holley Gerth is *The Wall Street Journal* bestselling author of *The Powerful Purpose of Introverts: Why the World Needs You to Be You*. She imagines a world where we all become who we're created to be, use our strengths to serve, and grow for a lifetime.

Dorina Lazo Gilmore-Young is passionate about helping women discover God's glory on life's unexpected paths. Dorina is a speaker, podcaster, and author of children's books, Bible studies, and a devotional. She and her husband are raising three brave daughters in central California.

Simi John was born in India and raised in Texas. She is married to Jayson, who serves as a lead pastor at their local church, and they have two children. Simi is a speaker and author. Her passion is to empower women to walk confidently in their God-given identity.

Tasha Jun is a Korean American melancholy dreamer, storyteller, community builder, wife to Matt, and mama to three. *Tell Me that Dream Again* is Tasha's compelling memoir-in-essays about identity and belonging.

Rachel Marie Kang is a writer of prose, poems, and other pieces. She is the author of *Let There Be Art* and *The Matter of Little Losses*. Rachel is the founder of The Follow House.

Aliza Latta is a Canadian pastor, artist, and author who is a huge fan of telling stories. She is always searching for the goodness of God, even when she has to squint to see it.

Jennifer Dukes Lee is the author of *Stuff I'd Only Tell God* and *Growing Slow*. She and her husband live on the fifth-generation Lee family farm in northwest Iowa, where they are raising crops, pigs, and two beautiful humans.

Kathi Lipp lives with her husband, Roger, and a bunch of chickens in the Sierra Nevada Mountains of California where they host writer retreats. She's a best-selling author and absolutely loves her Clutter Free Community on Facebook.

Jami Nato is an entrepreneur, leader, and author of *This Must Be the Place*. She is passionate about hoarding socks and not doing laundry, and loves using awkward humor and honesty to convey the truth of the gospel and navigate tough conversations.

Anjuli Paschall earned her master's degree in spiritual formation and soul care from Talbot Seminary and lives in Southern California with her husband (a pastor) and their five children. Anjuli is the author of *Stay and Awake*.

Anna E. Rendell works full-time for DaySpring from Minnesota, where she lives with her husband and four kids. Anna is the author of *A Moment of Christmas* and *Pumpkin Spice for Your Soul*, and co-author of *Take Heart* and *Empowered*.

Michelle Ami Reyes is an author and activist. Her first book, *Becoming All Things*, is the recipient of the 2022 ECPA award. Michelle writes at the intersection of multiculturalism, faith, and justice. She lives with her family in Austin, Texas.

Barb Roose is a speaker and author who is passionate about teaching women to live beautifully strong and courageous. She is the author of *Surrendered: Letting Go and Living Like Jesus*. Barb is a proud empty-nest mom of three, and prefers to eat dessert first.

Jen Schmidt loves to encourage, challenge, and cheer on women in both the beauty and bedlam of their everyday lives. A popular speaker, host of the Becoming conference, and author of *Just Open the Door*, Jen invites you to the joy of open-door living.

Kristen Strong, author of *When Change Finds You*, *Back Roads to Belonging*, and *Girl Meets Change*, writes as a friend helping you see a more hopeful view of your difficult life change. She and her US Air Force veteran husband, David, have three children.

Melissa Zaldivar is the host of the *Cheer Her On* podcast and author of *What Cannot Be Lost*. Melissa holds a master's degree in theology, and you can usually find her browsing in an antique store, leading tours at Orchard House, or walking along the coast of Massachusetts.

We hope you found peace, joy, and strength in your journaling experience.

Looking for more from the (in)courage community?

Visit their website at incourage.me and be sure to check out their entire collection at your favorite retailer or DaySpring.com.

Dear Friend,

This book was prayerfully crafted with you, the reader, in mind. Every word, every sentence, every page was thoughtfully written, designed, and packaged to encourage you—right where you are this very moment. At DaySpring, our vision is to see every person experience the life-changing message of God's love. So, as we worked through rough drafts, design changes, edits, and details, we prayed for you to deeply experience His unfailing love, indescribable peace, and pure joy. It is our sincere hope that through these Truth-filled pages your heart will be blessed, knowing that God cares about you—your desires and disappointments, your challenges and dreams.

He knows. He cares. He loves you unconditionally.

BLESSINGS!
THE DAYSPRING BOOK TEAM